ALAN TOMS

ALIVE TO GOD

GOOD ADVICE ON SEX, DATING AND DISCIPLESHIP FOR YOUNG CHRISTIANS

Contents

FOREWORD TO SECOND EDITION

Alan Toms was a full-time preacher and teacher among the churches of God. He engaged in pioneering gospel work in Burma (now Myanmar), India, North America and the UK, as well as teaching on 'Search for Truth' radio broadcasts for many years.

As a young teenager, I remember Alan coming to stay with our family in Northern Ireland while he visited our church. I admit to having been somewhat reluctant to give up my bedroom for this visitor! But I was to be rewarded by the man's disarming gentleness and genuine interest in our family. Alan left a hand-written letter of encouragement and challenge for me when he moved on; that letter was one of the most encouraging moments of my young life. Alan continued to be a source of encouragement and inspiration in the years that followed.

Soon after his visit to Northern Ireland, I remember picking up Alan's book, 'Alive unto God.' It was full of careful instruction for young people about topics that weren't often openly spoken about or discussed. Interest was maintained because of the 'edgy' topics Alan addressed! 'Alive unto God' would become one of my most-read books as a teenager, and one of my most-recommended books since (until stocks ran out!). Imagine my delight when I heard that work had begun to update 'Alive unto God'! Refreshing the content to bring it more up to date (society and culture have shifted a lot since Alan first wrote it) and updating the language were no small tasks, and we're very thankful for those who've contributed to the process and added insightful new material to supplement the original.

It's a joy to recommend this rejuvenated book to a new audience—both young and old—and I pray that the contents will be a real benefit to those who carefully read and refer to it, and to the updated list of recommended further reading at the back of the book.

"You who are young, be happy while you are young, and let your heart give you joy in the days of your youth. Follow the ways of your heart and whatever your eyes see, but know that for all these things God will bring you into judgment" (Ecclesiastes 11:9).

David Woods

BY WAY OF INTRODUCTION

A group of young campers sat around in a large tent. "We have a lot of questions," they said, "and many of them are about sex and marriage; not everyone is prepared to talk about these subjects; will you help us?" Their camp leader was young enough to remember his own teenage years and he wasn't afraid to face the issues. "Sure I will," he said, "provided you're willing to accept the answers the Bible gives." So they got started. Questions flowed thick and fast.

- "How can you be sure of God's guidance when you're looking for a husband or a wife?"
- "If you take a girl out, is it right to kiss?"
- "What about petting? Is it all OK for a Christian?"
- "I have a terrible job controlling my thoughts - can you help me?"
- "Does the Bible say anything about abortion?"

Darkness fell and they were still going. Someone went for a lamp. There was so much to talk about. Most young people feel the same, and the questions are urgent, demanding an answer. For this reason it was decided that something should be written, dealing frankly with the problems which face young people (though older people are not exempt) in today's world. They are good questions and it's right that they should be asked. It's equally right that they should be answered, and thankfully the Bible has the answers.

This is an attempt to bring the Word of God to deal with some of the problems which they were raising. I don't claim that what is written is the last word on any of the subjects; nor would every Bible-lover necessarily agree with each point that's made. With subjects like this, it may be difficult to reach full agreement on every detail. But I pray, and so do many others, that it may be helpful to some young people who press on so bravely for our Lord Jesus in a world which is so strongly opposed to all that's true and good.

Many of the subjects dealt with are intimate and personal, things which we might not find easy to discuss. But God speaks about them, and we are thankful He does. Indeed, the Bible is a remarkably frank book. The more we looked into the subject the more surprised we were to find how much God has to say about these intimate matters, and everything He says is straight and to the point. God sets His standards and sets them very high, as we would expect. But not so high that we cannot reach them. Thankfully, with His commands comes also His help to obey, and He has made wonderful provision to help us reach the standards He's set.

"Do you think it's rather prudish?" I asked a friend, after he'd read through some of the chapters. "Prudish?" he said, his eyebrows shooting upwards in surprise. "How can it be prudish if it's the Word of God?" How right he was. He hit the nail on the head. In that spirit we send it out. We write to young people who value the Word of God and are willing to face up to what it says, even if it does seem to be hitting hard. So we make no apologies for anything that's written. We recognize that if God is setting the standard it must be high. Lower it, we dare not. Aim at it, we must.

The earlier chapters are aimed at helping those who have recently come to know the Lord. Most of the case histories are from real experience, and so the names are changed in almost every case. One of my friends suggested that the book is too long; that young people will not take the time to wade through it. Maybe you'll prove him wrong! But even if you do go to the index and pick out the subjects which interest you specially, can I ask that you come back later and give the other chapters a browse over, along with your Bible, because there might be some points which you'll find helpful.

Before the manuscript was finalized, I asked some young people to suggest improvements and they came up with some most valuable ones. I'd like to acknowledge their help, and to say that it gave me a thrill to realise that there are young men and women in churches of God today, and not a few of them, who are serious about giving Christ their best. To them I send out my little book, very conscious of its limitations, but praying that it might help to strengthen the resolve of those who love our Lord Jesus, to daily count themselves dead to sin but ALIVE TO GOD IN CHRIST JESUS.

Alan Toms

1. LEARNING FROM THE YOUNG JESUS

"When he was twelve years old" (Luke 2:42).

"What's wrong with you this evening? You're a bit irritable, aren't you?" queried Andy's mother, when he got home from school. "Mum, you don't know what I'm up against. The boys talk about sex all the time, and they laugh at me when I don't join in." Poor Andy, he was having a rough time. He hadn't long been saved, and in his school it seemed as if he was all alone. He was really swimming against the tide for the first time in his life. Thankfully, he had parents at home who understood and it was helpful to be able to talk about it with them. Perhaps you don't live in that sort of home, which will make things even harder for you.

The fact that you are saved means that you're different, of course. Every young Christian has to get their heads around it. Before our conversion, we're swimming with the stream, and that's easy. But when we're saved we change direction. It's an about-turn; that's what conversion means. Everything is new for the Christian. *"If any man is in Christ, he is a new creature: the old has passed away; behold, the new has come"* (2 Corinthians 5:17): a new direction because we follow a new Master; a new sense of belonging, because we have a new Father in heaven; and a new power inside us, because of a new Friend living in our hearts, the Holy Spirit. It's all wonderful and exciting, but it makes us different from the rest, and we have to face up to it. We know it as soon as we're saved, but perhaps the full meaning of it only hits us when we're a teenager, because that's when the pressures really begin. And that's when a lot of life's important decisions are made.

MAKING DECISIONS

Don't you think it's important that the only reference we have in the Bible to Jesus from when he was born to when he was about 30 is one little episode when he was on the verge of becoming a teenager? It's certainly not an accident that Luke tells us of that visit to the Temple. With his medical knowledge from being a doctor, Luke knew as well as anybody how important that time is in a young person's life. One thing that's plain from this story is that this is the age when we start making decisions for ourselves.

The annual feast of the Passover had taken them up to Jerusalem, and when his parents left for home, he stayed behind. He wouldn't have done that when he was 8, or when he was 10, but now he was 12 and he was making responsible decisions for Himself. Not only did he decide to stay and learn from the teachers in the temple, but He'd made a far more important decision which comes out in His reply to his mother, when she found Him after her long search.

> *"Why were you looking for me? Did you not know that I must be in My Father's house?"* (Luke 2:49)

These words deserve our most careful attention, not just because they're the first words we have recorded of Jesus on earth, but also because they contain a principle which directed the rest of His life, and they will direct ours as well. That "must" gave direction to all the days that followed.

It was the first of many "musts," of course. "I must preach," "I must suffer," "I must go on my way today, tomorrow and the day following"; and that ominous "day following" was the day when he died at Calvary for our salvation. We know that he was God's Son and that He had come to die. We know also that as the Son of God he shared with His Father and with the Holy Spirit in determining, long before the world was made, how and when He would die. All that's true.

But here Luke is writing about Him as a boy, and at 12 He announced His decision. He had a Father in heaven and the doing of His will was to be the one and only purpose of His life. He must be in the things of His Father. And His Father is our Father; not in the unique way in which He was the Father of the Lord Jesus, of course, but nevertheless just as definitely. And there is nothing better than getting our priorities sorted out in early years and deciding what's going to be given first place in our lives. To a very large extent what we make of life will depend upon where we place our "musts."

FIRST THINGS FIRST

"Seek first the kingdom of God, and His righteousness; and all these things will be added to you," the Lord Jesus said, and this is the great text that has helped so many to get on course in life and to keep on it. We know that God's things ought to be given first place in our lives, but why? Such a sweeping statement must be supported by strong reasons. But here are three outstanding ones. Because God is our maker, and He has a claim upon us by right of being our Creator. Secondly, because Christ died to save us, and with His blood He has bought us for Himself; so we are not our own. Thirdly, because only the things of God are of lasting value. All other things pass away and therefore their value is limited. God's things alone are eternal, lasting for ever.

"Let me first ..." said one young man (Matthew 8:21). "No! God first," said the Lord Jesus, and if we make that decision God will look after the other things, which are the daily things of life. It's not that they are unimportant, far from it, but they must take second place if we are going to be anything for God. "You look after my things, and I will look after yours," is, in effect, what God says. It is the age-old principle: *"those who honour Me, I will honour"* (1 Samuel 2:30) and it is still true.

"When you're writing to young people, ask them not to neglect their church responsibilities for the sake of their studies, or for any other reason," said one of my friends. "I'm speaking from experience. God will look after the exams and everything else provided we work hard at other times and don't forget His things." It's a good point and a practical one. Many Christians who have got to the top of their professions have proved the same thing. *"Not neglecting to meet together, as is the habit of some ..."* (Hebrews 10:25) is a command to be obeyed, and God will take note of our obedience and honour us for it. If it is the evening of the church prayers, for example, and you're a disciple of the Lord Jesus, then you be there, throwing your heart and soul into it. And of course it goes without saying that no disciple ever willingly misses the meeting for the Breaking of the Bread.

ADVANCING ON COURSE

We get on course when we make our decision to put the "must" where the boy Jesus put His, and then we run hard, as hard as we can go. It says of the Lord Jesus that He *"increased in wisdom and stature, and in favour with God and man,"* (Luke 2:52) and that covers His teenage years and adolescence. Jesus *"increased,"* and the Revised Version of the Bible uses the word *"advanced."* It is a key word - it means "to strike forward." It might be used of a pioneer hacking down trees as he cuts his way through a forest. The Lord Jesus did that. In the workshop each day He learned to use His carpenter's tools until He became a master of His trade.

And at the same time His young mind was grappling with the law of God, and on that law He meditated day and night. There was no short-cut for Him any more than there is for us. He hacked His way forward. And so must we. We make our decision that the things of the Father are a "must" for us, and then we put all we have into this great task of training ourselves to become men and women of God.

We write to encourage our young friend Andy, and all the other young people who are starting out in the greatest life of all but finding the going tough at times. No-one knows better than you the problems you are up against, or the temptations that you face – except One, your Master in heaven. He was once a teenager and He faced the same problems and was victorious over them, for it says, *"He increased in favour with God and man"* (Luke 2:52). And now from heaven He calls you to follow where He has led the way. You have started out on a life which is worthwhile a thousand times over, even though the going may be hard at times.

I was at a school swimming gala recently, and one of the twelve-year-olds was in the water for the third time that evening. He'd won his first two events. The hundred metres free-style was called over the loudspeaker and at the crack of the gun he was in the water and forging ahead. Every muscle in his body seemed to be pulling toward the end of that pool. It was easy to see who his parents were. They could not keep still in their seats! He came in first again and what a welcome he received. I had to turn away. There was a lump in my throat. Young Christian, go to it for all you are worth. Strain every muscle for His sake who watches from on high. It will be worth it. God tells you it will.

2. CHRISTIAN HOME LIFE

"and he ... was submissive to them" (Luke 2:51).

Before we leave that lovely reference to the Lord Jesus at the age of twelve, let's learn one more lesson from it. As a boy He was one of a large family. He was unique, of course, in that He had no earthly father, conceived, as He was, by the power of the Holy Spirit; but His parents had other children, four sons of whom we know, and some daughters (see Mark 6:3). He grew up in that family circle, and He helped to make it the happy home it was.

We have already noticed that His complete devotion to His heavenly Father prompted Him to remain in Jerusalem when the rest of the family made for home, but this did not prevent Him from being subject to His earthly parents. Indeed, one of his Father's commands was, *"Honour your father and your mother"* (Exodus 20:12)! So when they found Him, it says, *"He went down with them, and came to Nazareth; and He was submissive to them."* How thankful we are that Luke told us this. The Lord Jesus has left us the perfect example as to how to balance the claims of the Lord with obedience to our parents. They go hand in hand; they must, for both are equally His will for us.

He went home to Nazareth to keep *"the first commandment with a promise"* as Paul describes it (Ephesians 6:2). The command is given, and then a marvelous promise added for all who obey. And please note it's carried over to the New Testament, so we can't escape it by saying we are not under the law of Moses! No, there it is, clear and plain, and it applies to every child and youth in every home. There is also a word to parents, so let us have a brief look at that - for after all home life begins with them.

THE SECRET OF A HAPPY HOME

"Wives, submit to your own husbands, as to the Lord." "Husbands, love your wives, even as Christ loved the church, and gave Himself up for her" (Ephesians 5:22,25). These are the two basic instructions for a happy home as it affects husbands and wives. There will not be disharmony when these two words are obeyed.

As you might know, the New Testament was written in Greek, and there are four Greek words for love. One refers exclusively to the love of parents for their children, and children for parents. Another, "eros," is confined to physical love, and is not used in the Bible at all. The two verbs most commonly used in the New Testament for "to love" are "phileo" and "agapao." "Phileo" refers to the sort of love which comes spontaneously, like the love of a mother for her child. It is a love that cherishes. Occasionally it is used of the love of God for His Son, and for us, but as a general rule when God's love is referred to, it is the noun "agape" which is used. This is the word God chose to describe a love which isn't only an emotion, but it's an act of the will, as Greek experts put it. For instance, when Jesus taught us to love our enemies He couldn't have used "phileo," for that love doesn't come naturally.

"Agape" was the only word that could describe this high kind of love which loves the unloveable. It takes the whole of a man to love like this, not only his heart, but his mind and will as well. Such love is a love that gives: *"For God so loved the world that He gave His only Son."* It is a love that suffers: *"Christ loved the church and gave Himself up for her."* And when God commands husbands to love their wives, 'agape' is the word He uses. He required nothing less than such love, a self-sacrificing love which never looks for any return. Is it possible? Yes, *"... because God's love has been poured into our hearts through the Holy Spirit who has been given to us"* (Romans 5:5).

When husbands truly love their wives with this sort of love, how much easier it is for wives to obey God's instruction to them, and to be subject to their husbands. And that undoubtedly is the foundation of a happy home. If you find yourself in that sort of a home where your parents are at least aiming at God's lovely standard, then thank God with all your heart. It gives you a tremendous start in life. But some may come from homes where their parents are not yet saved. Keep on praying for them, won't you, and ask God's help to live your life so that they will see the difference Christ makes.

And some may come from broken homes, where one of the parents has gone away. You ask, how does God's command affect me? Am I included in it? Yes, we're all in it, regardless of the sort of home we come from. *"Children, obey your parents in the Lord, for this is right"* is the verse in Ephesians (6:1), but in Colossians Paul words it differently: *"Children, obey your parents in everything, for this pleases the Lord"* (Colossians 3:20). It seems to me that the two verses take in both situations - those who have parents who are in the Lord, and those who do not. In all cases obedience is called for. The only exception I can think of is where unbelieving parents may ask a son or daughter to do something which is plainly against God's word - and if that happened they would need to explain in a respectful way why they could not obey.

AUTHORITY COMES FROM GOD

Why should children obey their parents? Because God has given their parents authority; to the father first, as head of the home, and then to the mother as joined with him. They have a God-given authority. Authority is not a very popular word today. I wonder what thoughts the word conjures up in your mind. All authority comes down from God above, for He is Lord of heaven and earth, and therefore it is absolutely good. He gives authority to rulers of nations to govern the people under them. He gives authority to overseers in churches of God to govern disciples of the Lord Jesus who are in the kingdom of God. And He gives authority to each father to control the family under his care. When that authority is acknowledged there is happiness and peace; when it is rebelled against there is lawlessness. And all kinds of harmful things follow where lawlessness exists.

"The mystery of lawlessness is already at work" (2 Thessalonians 2:7), the apostle said, and the world is full of evidence of that fact. "I'm my own boss and I can do as I please," is the attitude which sparks off so many problems. Is that right? Of course not! Very few are in the position of being their own boss and even those few will find someone above them, whose authority has to be acknowledged. That is the way God has arranged things, and it is for our good. If we bow to it we shall save ourselves many a heartache, and this is true at home as it is elsewhere. Obviously the Lord knew that there would be the tendency for fathers to get exasperated with their children, for He guided Paul to include that short verse, *"Fathers, do not provoke not your children, lest they become discouraged"* (Colossians 3:21). Fathers can become discouraged, and so can the children. It works both ways. I hope that some of the fathers will read this chapter and take note.

And then you will do your bit, won't you? Give your parents or guardians the credit for having lived a few years longer than you. Mark Twain once said, "When I was sixteen I thought my Dad was hopeless. When I was twenty, I was surprised to discover that he had made progress." When God says obey your parents in all things, He means *all things.* It is sweeping, but it is the way to a happy home life.

THE GENERATION GAP

Some people talk a lot about the generation gap as though it were a new thing! Twenty-odd years makes a difference in anyone's thinking, so there is bound to be some gap. We can hardly expect children and parents to always think the same way and it would be rather boring if they did! But there is no point in making the gap wider than it needs to be. Men who build bridges work from both ends and meet in the middle - and generation gaps can be bridged if both sides do their best to understand one another.

You remember Absalom? If not, read the story in 2 Samuel 13-19. He worked hard at widening the gap between his father and himself. He was a young prince and was brought up in the luxury of a palace. But that was his home and the same commandment was binding on him. He had a father who was one of the best. God said David was a man after His own heart (1 Samuel 13:14), so he must have been good. Strangely enough Absalom was against him. He thought he knew better than his father and although he had everything a prince could desire, he stole the hearts of the people and led them in revolt against the king. This was lawlessness at its worst. Pride was at the root of his trouble, of course.

He was a good-looking fellow and he knew it. The most handsome in his country, the Bible says. And his chief pride was his hair. He trimmed it once a year when he could bear the weight no longer. And God used that very thing to bring about his downfall, for fall he did. *"Pride goes before destruction, and a haughty spirit before a fall"* (Proverbs 16:18). The battle went against him in the end. Absalom tried to escape on his mule, but his head caught in the branches of a great oak tree. His mule ran on, but he was left hanging. He hung for a good while, too. He was still alive when Joab came and thrust three darts through his heart. I wonder what his thoughts were as he hung from that tree? Did he remember the day when he started to go wrong? If only ... but it was too late now. Death was staring him in the face.

HEED GOOD ADVICE

To one of Absalom's half-brothers David once said, *"... my son, know the God of your father and serve him with a whole heart and with a willing mind, for the Lord searches all hearts and understands every plan and thought. If you seek him, he will be found by you, but if you forsake him, he will cast you off forever. Be careful now ..."* (1 Chronicles 28:9-10). Had he never said something similar to Absalom? Surely he had. But Absalom had taken no notice. Other things riled his thoughts. He calculated it would be better getting his own way. Two sons of the same father, the one accepted instruction, the other didn't. The one who did, Solomon, became an excellent father himself and some of the most honest advice given to any sons came from his pen (see Proverbs and Ecclesiastes).

That's the way God intends it should be, from father to son, from father to son. If you are now at the "son" (or daughter) stage, take the advice. One day you may be filling the "father" or "mother" role and be desperately anxious then that your son or daughter listens to you. Here is some of the advice Solomon gave:

"Hear, my son, your father's instruction, and forsake not your mother's teaching ... My son, if sinners entice you, do not consent. If they say, Come with us ... My son, do not walk in the way with them; hold back your foot from their paths, for their feet run to evil, and they make haste to shed blood" (Proverbs 1:8,10,11,15,16).

We can't say it's out of date, can we? Quick to shed blood – isn't that true wherever there's lawlessness? God's Word never grows old. Here is more:

"My son, do not forget my teaching, but let your heart keep my commandments, for length of days and years of life and peace they will add to you. Let not steadfast love and faithfulness forsake you; bind them around your neck; write them on the tablet of your heart. So you will find favor and good success in the sight of God and man. Trust in the LORD with all your heart, and do not lean on your own understanding. In all your ways acknowledge him, and he will make straight your paths. Be not wise in your own eyes; fear the LORD, and turn away from evil" (Proverbs 3:1-7).

And so we could go on, for there is so much wise instruction in the early chapters of the Proverbs. Read it for yourself and translate the advice into your daily living, and it will keep you straight. And when you become a father, or a mother, in the will of God, you will be far better equipped to guide your own sons and daughters if you've lived by the same rules yourself.

3. OUR BODIES

**_"Do you not know that your body is a temple of the Holy Spirit?"_ (1
Corinthians 6:19)**

"How far should I get involved in school sports?" That was the problem.
Jake was good at all kinds of sport, very good, including soccer. He was
all set for the school team, but that would mean most Saturdays occupied
during the season and even an occasional game on Sunday. Jake knew
that this was not for him as a young disciple, but how far could he go
without getting too involved? Was there any guidance for him in this?

"_... while bodily training is of some value; godliness is of value in every way,
as it holds promise for the present life, and also for the life to come_" (1
Timothy 4:8) wrote Paul to Timothy. Yes, Jake remembered that verse.
It certainly seemed to be connected to the subject. The sports on the
school curriculum definitely provided bodily exercise, and if God said
such exercise had some value, then sports had their usefulness. It was
good training in working as a team, too, a most important lesson in life.
But thinking over the verse again Jake could see that the "little" was set
in contrast to the "all things," and clearly Paul intended the one should
be balanced against the other. The young Christian has prior claims upon
him, stronger and more urgent than the claims of sport – the claims of
God.

SPORT

This was the point Paul made to the Corinthians. They knew about sport better than most, for the Olympic games originated in their country and were still a regular feature when Paul wrote, and for years afterwards. You can almost hear the runner pounding down the track as Paul wrote of him striving in the games. What was he after? A laurel crown, that was all. And that soon faded. True, there was the satisfaction and glory of winning, but that faded, too, for the world soon forgets. Paul was in a race greater by far, and so are we if we have been baptised and have started to follow the Lord Jesus.

And if someone happens to be reading this who is saved but not yet baptized, maybe Jake's experience will help you. He was still unbaptized and he felt shy about it, for he knew he ought to be baptized. They had a missionary coming to tea with them and Jake wondered if there would be any awkward conversations. But the missionary was not out to make the young chap feel awkward. He just waited for his opportunity, and when the conversation turned to sport at school, he leaned over to him and said, "You can't start running until you are in the race, Jake, can you?" "No, Mr. Atkinson, that's true," and looking up, he noticed a twinkle in his eye. Jake got the point. He knew the Bible likened the discipleship life to a race (see 1 Corinthians 9:24; Hebrews 12:1) and surely baptism is the starting point. He decided he would delay no longer. Maybe you will take the point, too, and follow the psalmist's good example. He said, "*I hasten, and do not delay to keep your commandments*" (Psalm 119:60).

Having got into the race, we will then need to keep fit if we are to run well. "*Train yourself for godliness*" (1 Timothy 4:7), wrote Paul. "Gymnasium" yourself. That's the Greek word, and every gymnast knows you cannot afford to let up, even for one day. Nor do we want to, for the race we are in affects not only this life, but also the life which is to come. We are running with eternity in view. Jake got his problem sorted out fortunately, and he decided that anything which might get in the way of doing the Lord's work was out as far as he was concerned. Many of his Saturdays were occupied anyway with conventions, youth events and outreach work, so there was no time for the school team. He was glad really, for he knew it would involve him in other things which it would be questionable for a young disciple to engage in.

YOGA

"My friend has offered to teach me yoga," said Hannah excitedly when she got home from school one day. It sounded attractive, for Hannah was a keen gymnast. Every patch of grass was an invitation to spin a cartwheel. "Be careful, Hannah, for there can be more to yoga than exercises, you know." Yoga comes from India and has sprung out of the Hindu religion, which is completely opposed to the teaching of the Bible. In yoga the exercise of the body is linked with meditation that is supposed to bring the body under control. But that is not God's way of controlling the body. The Holy Spirit has come to live in *our* hearts, and one of the great reasons why He has come is to help us control our bodies. There is a most interesting verse which says, *"If the Spirit of him who raised Jesus from the dead dwells in you, he who raised Christ Jesus from the dead will also give life to your mortal bodies through his Spirit who dwells in you"* (Romans 8:11).

This is something which should happen every day of our lives, the Holy Spirit "giving life" to us so that our bodies can be yielded to the Lord for Him to use. This is a promise for every Christian, young and old and in-between, and covers every part of our lives. The Holy Spirit lives within to give us power to overcome sin and to live happy and victorious lives.

"Reigning in life through Jesus Christ" is the way Paul describes it (Romans 5:17). It sounds good, doesn't it? Yes, but let us not be content with the sound of it. This is something real, to be experienced and enjoyed every day, so we go through school and college and into our first job as young people to whom the Holy Spirit is a living reality, a Friend and Helper who has come to live in our hearts for the express purpose of helping us in every experience of life.

DRUGS

When this is the case there is no need for uppers, pills to give that extra spurt when the final exams are coming up. The Holy Spirit indwells to give us life. The young Christian who appreciates this makes their exams a subject for special prayer and asks for the Holy Spirit's help to do his best. God loves to answer that sort of prayer. Look up John 14:13 for the reason. In regard to uppers (and downers), keep off them anyway, please. For many a young person has got into the habit and been led on to the more harmful drugs. Or perhaps they have started on drugs just for "kicks," little realizing the tremendous danger involved.

There is danger, dreadful danger, and the number of young people who are ruining their lives through drugs is rapidly on the increase. If you are in any doubt about the subject get hold of one of the good books listed in the bibliography and read the evidence supplied by men who devote their lives to trying to help young people who have been hooked on drugs. A hard task they have, for many are beyond the reach of help. Their bodies wasted and their brains weakened, they just wait to die a pitiable death. And what of their precious souls? Drug-taking is a worldwide menace.

Those who push drugs say that some are not habit-forming. Do not believe them. For medical experts are warning that some of the soft drugs, as they are called, are more damaging in their effect in some ways than the hard drugs. So be warned and beware! There are evil people around who traffic in drugs and their business is to get into contact with young people, particularly. They make money out of destroying young lives and behind them of course, is really the Destroyer himself. *"The thief"* the Lord Jesus called him, and He said he *"comes only to steal and kill and destroy"* (John 10:10). He knows his time is short and he is working furiously today. Keep absolutely clear of all types of drugs yourself, and if you know any friends who are getting involved, whether Christians or not, warn them of the danger.

One day, perhaps sooner than we think, we shall each stand before the Judgment Seat of Christ, and the Bible says we are going to receive what is due for the things done in the body, whether it be good or bad (2 Corinthians 5:10). That will be a solemn time when we give account to the Lord Jesus of how we have used our bodies. The tendency today is for more leisure time. Less work and more time off. Let us make sure we use our leisure to profit and put the members of our bodies to good use for our Master. Note it is for good or bad. The Devil will not be slow to introduce us to bad things if we do not diligently fill our time with the good.

MASTURBATION

"What about masturbation?" asked one young person. "Do you think the Lord would include it among the bad things we might do with our bodies?" Yes, I do, and it is something which is done in private, so unless we are on our guard, we might easily fall into the habit. It affects boys and girls, of course, the handling of one's own private parts to give sexual pleasure. I believe the Bible touches on this subject when it says, *"that each one of you know how to control his own body in holiness and honor, not in the passion of lust like the Gentiles who do not know God"* (1 Thessalonians 4:4-5).

What we do in private God sees and knows, and *"love that issues from a pure heart, and a good conscience and a sincere faith"* (1 Timothy 1:5) is something God wants us all to aim for. Nobody can masturbate with a good conscience, can they? As we shall see in a later chapter, God intends us to have sexual pleasure when joined in marriage with the partner of our choice, and masturbation is a poor substitute for that. So if you happen to have got into the habit, ask God's help to get clear of it, and share your intention with an accountability partner. And then set God's high standard before you: *"Whatever you do, in word or in deed, do everything in the Name of the Lord Jesus, giving thanks to God the Father through Him"* (Colossians 3:17).

HOMOSEXUALITY

While on such subjects, let us raise a warning note about the practice of homosexuality, which is sexual behaviour between persons of the same sex, whether men or women. Once a punishable offence, the laws of many countries now allow it, for example, between consenting adults. But that doesn't make it any less sinful in God's sight, of course. And the fact that the occurrence is on the increase today means that we need to be alert to the seriousness of it.

We must understand the difference, though, between the sexual activity itself and the sexual desires which some people feel towards persons of the same sex, which are termed "same sex attraction." Many people are in this position through no fault of their own; it may be the result of a development in this area of their personality, as a consequence of the fallen nature. It would be wrong for sin to be attributed to such a person so long as he or she doesn't disobey the Scriptures in satisfying such desires with persons of the same sex. In this, their situation is like that of a person who is attracted to the opposite sex and who obeys God's word about abstaining from sexual immorality or impurity, maintaining chastity in honour to the Lord's command.

But let's be clear that acting on homosexual urges is totally wrong to God. It distorts what God wants to see in human relationships and he condemns it strongly. *"You shall not lie with a male, as with a woman; it is an abomination"* (Leviticus 18:22). And you will notice that His condemnation of it affects all men, not only believers: *"For this reason God gave them up to dishonorable passions. For their women exchanged natural relations for those that are contrary to nature; and the men likewise gave up natural relations with women and were consumed with passion for one another, men committing shameless acts with men and receiving in themselves the due penalty for their error"* (Romans 1:26-27). Such serious sin brings its own consequences, but we don't keep clear just for that reason. The Christian has a much higher reason than that for keeping himself from sin. His body is a temple of the Holy Spirit, and every day that dawns is a fresh opportunity of glorifying God in that body. God's Word is clear about the context and environment for the enjoyment of sex – between a married man and woman, in the privacy of their own life-setting. Any sexual activity straying beyond God's boundaries is forbidden.

"HAVE I NOT A LIFE TO GIVE?

"Have I not a life to give?" asked a young African leprous man, as pleadingly he looked into the face of his missionary friend. He wanted to run on in front, through the bush, to make sure the way was clear. He could not do much with his poor, clawed hands, but he could still run and that he wanted to do. A life to give? Yes, and for most of us it is in a healthier and perhaps more usable body than our African friend had to offer. To give or not to give? That is the question. What shall we do with our bodies, so wonderfully made, and with so great potential for either good or bad? Oh, how can we be sure of harnessing all their powers and capabilities for the glory of God? Paul has the answer: *"I appeal to you therefore, brothers, by the mercies of God, to present your bodies a living sacrifice, holy, acceptable to God, which is your spiritual worship"* (Romans 12:1). Who is willing to do that?

WHAT WE WEAR

Then the apostle went on to say, *"Do not be conformed to this world"* (Romans 12:2) and that has to do with the body, too, the way we dress it up (the Revised Version translates it as *"the fashion of this world"*). The world is always looking for something new, and so fashions quickly change. But the Christian is not called to be in the height of fashion. In regard to what we wear, Peter gets right to the point when he writes about women's outward adorning, for he uses the very word for "adorning" which is normally translated "world." There is no doubt that fashions belong to the world, and nowadays they attract the male world almost as much as the female. Let the world have its fashions. We have Christ.

As far as what we wear is concerned, we do not aim at the latest fashion, but we don't want to be conspicuous the other way. But whatever we wear let it be modest, for that is the plain word of the Lord. *"I desire ... that women adorn themselves in respectable apparel"* (1 Timothy 2:8-9). And I believe that this applies even in what we wear on the beach. Let's not draw attention to our bodies by what we wear, or the lack of it. That isn't right for a follower of Christ. Is that too hard a knock at the end of a chapter? It shouldn't be, for the Lord's young men and women who are really serious about pleasing Him. God made the first clothing both for the man and his wife, in Eden, and He obviously intended us to be properly covered. *"Whatever you do, do all to the glory of God"* (1 Corinthians 10:31).

4. OUR MINDS

"Set your mind on the things that are above, not on things that are on the earth" **(Colossians 3:2).**

"It's only a game," some of them said. But was it? The expression on their faces suggested It was more than a game. Suspicion, alarm, fear … they were all there, written on the faces of a group of teenagers sitting around a table, and in the centre was a 'ouija board.' For some it was the first time they had seen it used and the way the board came up with the answers was frightening, to say the least. And well it might be. For those who have studied the use of the Ouija board are in no doubt that this is one of the things which Satan is using to capture the minds of people today. The manufacturers of the board state in their sales brochure that how or why it works is a mystery. And of course Satan likes to keep it that way, but to Bible students it is no mystery. We recognise it as another form of the occult to which so many are being increasingly attracted. Occult means 'hidden' and these are Satan's hidden things which he uses to draw the minds of men and women far away from God.

THE OCCULT

You may well run up against it at school or in the University, for some education authorities are offering the occult, witchcraft and magical arts as subjects for higher study. If you do come across it, be sure to keep completely clear, for these are the deep things of Satan, as the Bible says. Do not allow curiosity to make you enquire into it.

> *"And when they say to you, "Inquire of the mediums and the necromancers who chirp and mutter," should not a people inquire of their God? Should they inquire of the dead on behalf of the living? To the teaching and to the testimony! If they will not speak according to this word, it is because they have no dawn"* (Isaiah 8:19-20).

And if there is no morning that means that it is all night, all darkness. What a fearful thing for those who refuse God's word, and give place to the Devil. There is only the blackness of darkness for ever. Those who traffic in these things are after the young. They have been since Isaiah's day - take a note of Isaiah 47:12,15. But we can clearly see that this is something from which we must keep far away. *"To the law and to the testimony,"* cried God's prophet (Isaiah 8:20). Good words these. Yes, we shall be safe if we keep close to God's Word, and in regard to the occult His Word could not be plainer:

> *"There shall not be found among you anyone who burns his son or his daughter as an offering, anyone who practices divination or tells fortunes or interprets omens, or a sorcerer or a charmer or a medium or a necromancer or one who inquires of the dead, for whoever does these things is an abomination to the Lord"* (Deuteronomy 18:10-12).

That list surely covers every form of the occult. The whole thing belongs to Satan, and let us not be afraid to stand up and say so.

MINDFULNESS AND MEDITATION

"Yes, I agree with all that," you say, "but what about mindfulness and meditation?" People claim it relaxes the mind and lifts it out of the frustrations of materialism into a new freshness and creativity." Do not be deceived, please, by any meditation that is far removed from what the Bible teaches. The blessed man of Psalm 1 meditated in the law of God, his mind roving over the wonders of God's Word and works (see Psalm 143:5,6). This is so different from the empty mind and the suspended thought which we hear so much of today.

But it all goes to show that Satan is after the mind. "The battle is in the mind," one of my Bible teachers used to say, and how right he was. If the Adversary can get control of our minds he has won the battle. And, of course, he is after the mind of the believer as well as the unbeliever. Which only emphasises the importance of what Paul wrote to the Corinthians: *"The weapons of our warfare are not of the flesh, but mighty before God to the casting down of strong holds; casting down imaginations, and every high thing that is exalted against the knowledge of God, and bringing every thought into captivity to the obedience of Christ"* (2 Corinthians 10:5).

STRONGHOLDS AGAINST GOD

Students who go in for higher education have to be specially on their guard, for they sit at the feet of some of the master minds of their countries. If their professors and lecturers happen to be men and women who question the authority of the Bible then the stage is all set for a battle.

And behind the stage (and often out of sight) is the great Enemy himself, keenly interested in what is happening. Where is the battle? It is in the mind of the young Christian. The things he is asked to believe are high things indeed, strongly supported by the highest intellectual thought, but in many cases they are exalted against the knowledge of God. What is the young Christian to do? Thank God He has not left us defenceless. The weapons of our warfare are as effective today as when our Master Himself was under attack. Taking up the sword of the Spirit, God's Word, He used it strong and well. *"It is written"* He said and against that the Enemy had no defence.

Take it up, young Christian, and do not be afraid. And with it take up the large shield of faith. Never allow any doubts about the authority of the Bible to linger in your mind. There are a lot of very intelligent and educated people who are also committed Christians and they find no conflict between the established facts of science and what the Bible teaches. Line yourself up with them, and go on strongly for the Lord.

Christ in you, that is the hope of glory. And when Christ comes in, He comes to take control of every part of our lives, including our thought life. When we get saved our minds are renewed. That is something the Holy Spirit does. Previously we could not understand the things of God. They were foolishness to us (see 1 Corinthians 2:14). But now we can, and the Holy Spirit who searches the deep things of God takes pleasure in revealing them to us. Has it ever dawned on you that your mind could be filled with the very thoughts which fill the mind of God? That the things about which the Father and the Son and the Holy Spirit speak together, They want to share with you? This is a tremendous truth, but we can see that one condition must be fulfilled - every thought must be brought into captivity to the obedience of Christ.

CONTROLLING OUR THOUGHTS

Our thoughts so quickly run loose, as David found that evening he walked on his roof-top. He ought not to have been there at all for it was at *"the time when kings go out to battle"* (2 Samuel 11:1), and he should have been with his men, leading them to victory. Instead he was at home, and the Devil was gaining the victory over him. Where was the battle? In the mind, as it always is. He saw a woman bathing and unclean thoughts came into his mind. What should he have done? Rejected them immediately, and replaced them with thoughts of God's Word. But instead he fed his mind upon them, and thoughts led to actions which David bitterly regretted for the rest of his life.

It is true that God forgave him when he repented and confessed his sin, but he carried with him some of the bitter results all his days, and sadly so did others, for his sin affected more lives than just his. *"Each person is tempted when he is lured and enticed by his own desire. Then desire when it has conceived gives birth to sin, and sin when it is fully grown brings forth death"* (James 1:14-15).

That is what happened in David's case, and it all began with his thoughts. How can we keep out evil thoughts which do so much harm, and rob us of fellowship with God? How can we keep our minds holy and clean? When God gave instructions about clean things in Leviticus 11, He said *"a spring or a cistern holding water shall be clean"* (Leviticus 11:36), simply because if it was full of water it could not be full of other things as well. Surely there is no other way of keeping our minds clean than by filling them with clean things, and this we do by a deliberate, positive action of our will: *"Finally, brothers, whatever is true, whatever is honorable, whatever is just, whatever is pure, whatever is lovely, whatever is commendable, if there is any excellence, if there is anything worthy of praise, think about these things"* (Philippians 4:8).

Are you having a problem controlling your thoughts? And do you really want to get to grips with it? Begin today by committing this lovely verse to memory, and take another each day, and fill your mind with the pure Word of God, and you will be well on your way to becoming an overcomer. *"I have stored up your word in my heart, that I might not sin against you"* (Psalm 119:11).

5. SEX

"Male and female created He them" (Genesis 1:27).

Some Christians never refer to the subject of sex except in whispers, as though it was not something that should be really talked about. On the other hand, many in the world have no problem talking about it, but often in the wrong way by treating something that is special as common, or by making it part of a dirty joke. We must not join them in this, of course, for filthiness, foolish talking and joking are among the things which Paul says _"must not even be named among you, as is proper among saints"_ (Ephesians 5:3). And we are saints if we believe on the Lord Jesus – a 'saint' is a person whom God has set apart in Christ from the rest of the world, and having been made a saint we are responsible to live saintly lives.

With this in mind let us have a straight look together at the subject of sex and see what God has to say about it in His Word. At once let it be plainly said that sex is NOT a dirty subject. It is something pure and wholesome, for God Himself has designed it, part of His creative work, and all that He has done is good. When He began the human race He first created a man and then made a woman. _"Male and female He created them,"_ because He knew so well that they would need one another. What a strange sort of world this would be if all human beings were males, or all females!

GOD-GIVEN DESIRE

When God made the first man and woman He put into them both an appetite for sexual activity. This is a normal, healthy thing, just as our appetite for food, or our desire for sleep. The food instinct reveals itself almost as soon as a baby is born for it cries for milk. But the sex instinct does not make itself so strongly felt until young people reach puberty, usually between twelve and fourteen years of age. At this period in our lives we begin to take notice of one another, and at first we may feel a bit shy about it. This is normal. It would be strange if it wasn't like this, as strange as a baby not wanting any food. But like all other instincts it has to be controlled. Some babies would keep on eating everything within their reach if their mothers did not know when they had had enough and quietly remove food from them. Babies have gradually to learn to control their appetites.

The sexual desires which we begin to feel in our early teens for members of the opposite sex are God-given, so we don't need to be afraid of them. But we have to learn to control our sexual desires. Their great purpose, as we shall see, is in married life, but how are we to cope with these desires during our teens and until we get married? That is the vital question to which we seek an answer from God's Word. The sex instinct is powerful used according to His instructions it works for our highest good. But it can lead to the lowest depths of degradation and despair if it's misused.

Like fire it is a wonderful servant, but if fire gets out of control it results in havoc! We live in a world which is becoming increasingly obsessed with sex. It has got out of control and is running wild. Broken homes, unmarried mothers, one-parent families and the self-destroying use of pornography are just a few of the heart-breaking results which we see all around us. And many people are suffering from sexually transmitted diseases which come as a result of disregarding God's holy laws in regard to sex. And if that's true in their bodies, what about their minds? It is all some people think and talk about, and the great Adversary sees to it that they get plenty on television and online to keep their minds fed. It is the old story. The Devil has got hold of one of God's finest gifts which God intended only for our good and happiness, perverted it through sin, and used it to bring many to the depths of deepest despair.

DISCIPLINE REQUIRED

Uncontrolled sex was the cause of Samson's downfall. If ever a young man had a promising start it was Samson. Born into a godly home, with parents who asked God's special help in bringing him up, everything was set for a useful, prosperous and God-honouring life. Samson was one of God's Nazirites, someone specially set apart for God and for His service. But early in life he failed to discipline himself on this very subject which we're considering. Samson went down to the Philistine's country, saw a woman and fell in love with her. *"Get her for me,"* he said to his father, *"for she is right in my eyes"* (Judges 14:3).

Samson was a Hebrew, and his father was right when he protested that he should choose one of his own people to be his wife, but Samson wouldn't take advice. He thought he knew better than his father. Nor did he take any notice when God sent a young lion to roar against him and turn him home again. He wanted this girl and he would have her no matter what anyone said. Read his story in the 13th to 16th chapters of Judges and you will find that she was only one of three women who came into his life, and the last was the worst of the lot. Her name was Delilah, which means "enfeebling" (to weaken) and she brought Samson right down until, robbed of all his strength and his eyes gouged out, he spent the rest of his life in the Philistines' prison house.

Poor, blind Samson, if only he had got himself under control when he was young, what a different story his might have been! *"Flee youthful passions,"* wrote Paul to Timothy, *"and pursue righteousness, faith, love and peace, along with those who call on the Lord from a pure heart"* (2 Timothy 2:22). Temptations will come to every one of us, and sexual temptations are probably the strongest of all. Safety lies in flight! In other words, get out of the way of them as fast as you can. Surely that's what the Lord Jesus meant when He taught us to pray, *"And lead us not into temptation but deliver us from evil"* (Matthew 6:13). Keep us from places and situations where temptation will be strong. We need to pray that prayer every day. And if we pray it, then of course we must not put ourselves into such situations.

OUR FRIENDSHIPS

This brings us to the important question of boy/girl friendships. Are they right for disciples of the Lord Jesus, and if so, to what extent? In my judgement Christian young people are wiser to be friendly with all rather than single out one boy or girl for a special friendship, until such time as they have serious thoughts about the person concerned and feel that God may be indicating this person as their life partner. Love is a many-splendoured thing, someone has said, and certainly it is far deeper and nobler than just physical attraction. If we genuinely love a person we will not want that person to be hurt in any way. If we single out one of the opposite sex and date them before we have any definite thought of marriage, it may leave a deep hurt if later we drop the person. True love never does that.

"But how can we get to know a person well enough to be sure we want to marry if we never go out alone?" That is a sensible question. We must not overlook the importance of God's guidance, of course, which is discussed in a later chapter, and the fact that so often He puts a "feeling" in a person's heart, so that they have no doubt who their partner is to be.

But admittedly that doesn't always happen, and we must take a realistic look at this problem for the sake of those who feel that the only way to get to know one another sufficiently well is to date. If that's the case, play safe and have an honest and open understanding between you as to the level of your friendship. Other questions are immediately raised. To what extent can I show my affection? What about petting? Is it right for a Christian and, if so, how far can I go? These are delicate questions, and I can only advise what I believe to be a safe course for young disciples who are committed to their Master and who genuinely do not want to do anything to displease Him. There is *"a time to embrace, and a time to refrain from embracing"* (Ecclesiastes 3:5), said one experienced lover, and he was a man to whom God gave an extra amount of wisdom, so his words are especially worth pondering.

PETTING

To the average person in this world, a kiss means little or nothing, and some Christians exchange them freely without much thought. But others feel more strongly about it, and some would even go so far as to prefer to keep their first kiss for the person they really want to marry. But I agree that most people would consider that an extreme view, and I think we would need to distinguish between a goodnight kiss after an evening together and a passionate embrace, arousing strong feelings which are difficult to control. I am certain that if young people embrace to the point where they arouse one another's passions they are on very dangerous ground. They are exposing themselves to temptation and how can they then sincerely pray, *"Lead me not into temptation"*? And remember, girls, that boys are more quickly aroused than you are. Therefore, be specially careful not to allow your boyfriend to take any liberties with you, which you know would displease the Lord.

"Younger women as sisters, in all purity" (1 Timothy 5:2), was the instruction to Timothy as to how to behave towards the opposite sex. *"Younger men as brothers"* (1 Timothy 5:1), is God's instruction to young sisters. In other words, we treat them with no more familiarity than we would our own sisters or brothers, and with equal respect. "That's a hard line," you say. "Surely God knows that I feel differently about someone else's sister than I do about my own!" He does indeed, and that very feeling He has put into your make-up, just another of His precious gifts. You can enjoy it now, and benefit from the friendship that it leads you into, but remember that desire has to be controlled and maybe for a long time yet. For most young people, studies have to be completed and a steady job found before marriage can be considered, and rightly so. Therefore, for our own sakes it is wise not to arouse passions which cannot be fully satisfied, within the will of God, for many years to come.

"But what about after engagement? Can't we be more free with one another then?" It's true that the period of engagement is an opportunity for getting to know one another in readiness for marriage, but it doesn't give licence to 'get familiar.' We have already agreed that sex is one of God's special gifts, but in His wisdom He has commanded that it is reserved for marriage. *"Therefore shall a man leave his father and his mother and shall cleave unto his wife: and they shall be one flesh."* And then it says (please note when) after they were married, *"And the man and his wife were both naked, and were not ashamed"* (Genesis 2:24-25). In my judgement this cuts out what is sometimes called "heavy petting," the physical handling of one another's bodies, and that applies after engagement as well as before. Only after marriage is that allowed. Young Christian, take notice. Do not take liberties which will give you a guilty conscience and spoil your fellowship with God.

"But it's hard to wait. We love one another so much!" True, this requires discipline and self-control. But that is something we need to learn anyway. We shall require it after marriage as well as before. God knows the need and He has not left us to tackle the problem alone: *"God gave us a spirit not of fear; but of power and love and self-control"* (2 Timothy 1:7). *"The fruit of the Spirit is love, joy, peace ... self-control"* (Galatians 5:22-23).

God has provided for us in giving us the Holy Spirit, and if we allow Him to have His way in our hearts, He will produce in us that discipline which we require. And this is where true love shows itself for what it is. It is a selfish, immature love which cannot wait. Children behave like that. If they see something they want, they want it at once. True love considers what is best for the one loved, and a young couple who really love one another will be prepared to wait. But more about this subject in the next chapter.

6. SELF-CONTROL

"Keep yourself pure" (1 Timothy 5:22).

If Samson is God's great warning to young people of a life that was ruined because he gave in to temptation, Joseph is the outstanding example of a young man who triumphed over it. And he was young, too - only seventeen when he was torn away from his father and his home and sold into a rich man's house in a foreign land. But God was with him. *"The LORD is with you, while you are with Him"* (2 Chronicles 15:2) said Azariah the prophet. Yes, that was why God was with him, because Joseph was with God. He called on the Lord out of a pure heart and righteousness, faith, love and peace were the things he followed after. That didn't mean he was immune from temptation. Far from it. Right there where he was serving God and serving his master so faithfully and everything seemed to be going so well, temptation hit him as hard as it has ever hit any young man.

SAYING "NO"

Please read Genesis 39 carefully. *"His master's wife cast her eyes on Joseph, and said 'Lie with me'"* (v.7). But he refused. Full credit to him. And every day the temptation came. Not many have to face it so persistently as Joseph did. But he never yielded. Did Joseph not have any sexual feelings?

Of course he did. He was made the same way as all other young men. But to Joseph the God of heaven was real, and living and close at hand, and God made him strong to say "No." The Bible says so. *"His arms were made agile* [strong], *by the hands of the Mighty One of Jacob ... by the God of your father, who will help you"* (Genesis 49:24-25). God had helped him all these days and He was right there by his side to help him when this tough temptation came. *"How then can I do this great wickedness, and sin against God?"* he said, in reply. Tremendous words, aren't they? It was great wickedness in Joseph's view. Living in Egypt had not altered his standards. He was God's man wherever he was.

But if he had given in no one would have known, for on that final day there was no one else in the house. It is not likely his master's wife would ever have told. And in any case wouldn't it have been easier to give in, just this once, for the sake of keeping the peace? Ah, that is the way the Devil argues. Thank God Joseph didn't give in. If no one else was looking, God was, and that was what mattered to Joseph. When there was no other way to keep himself pure, he ran for it. Better to lose his coat and lose his job than lose a good conscience before God! And what was the end of Joseph's story? He became second in command over all of Egypt! *"Those that honour Me I will honour"* (1 Samuel 2:30), and when God honours a man or a woman, He does it well, doesn't He?

LIVING VICTORIOUSLY

Young Christian, *"keep yourself pure."* That was advice written to a young man and it has never been bettered. But let us be practical. How does a young Christian keep himself or herself pure in a world that is so impure? How do we live clean and think clean when we are living in a world that is a cesspool of sin? When every day at school and in college we are bombarded by so many things that are filthy? Let me say at once there is no easy answer, nor is there any instant prescription that will last for all time. This is something which is going to go on all through life and even older men and women get their temptations. It's something we have to face every day, and every day get the victory with the Lord's help. *"If anyone would come after Me, let him deny himself, and take up his cross daily, and follow Me"* (Luke 9:23), the Master said. It is a daily cross, and a cross is for dying on. Sinful desires spring out of the old nature and every day of our lives we have to ask God's help to consider that as dead. *"Consider yourselves dead to sin, alive to God in Christ Jesus"* (Romans 6:11). Other Christians before us have received God's help in living victorious lives, so why shouldn't we?

BIBLE READING

Can we find out what has helped them? Consistent, daily Bible reading would certainly come at the top of the list. *"How can a young man* [or woman] *keep his way pure? By guarding it according to your word"* (Psalm 119:9) The Word of God is a cleansing agent. *"The washing of water with the word"* (Ephesians 5:26), is the way Paul describes it. If we jealously guard our time alone with God each day and read and meditate in God's Word, it will have a cleansing and purifying effect in our lives and it will also strengthen us against temptation. Of course it is not enough to hurriedly read a few verses, close the book and dash off. We must treat the time seriously, put other things from our minds and come to our Bibles expecting God to speak to us. To keep a note-book handy is an excellent practice, and make notes of the lessons we learn; any verse which particularly impresses us, a promise we can claim, a warning to be heeded, or a command to be obeyed. In that way the precious Word of God will get into our hearts, and that will keep us from sin. *"I have stored up your word in my heart, that I might not sin against you"* (Psalm 119:11).

PRAYER

And of course linked with Bible study is prayer - that is always the case. The two go together. It is a two-way communication. God speaks to us when we read His Word, and we speak to Him when we kneel in prayer. Do not forget the kneeling. *"Let us kneel before the LORD our Maker: for He is our God"* (Psalm 95:6-7). That is why we kneel, because God is our Maker. *"Draw nigh to God, and He will draw nigh to you"* (James 4:8), said James in his short-and-sweet way. God near to us – what a tremendous thought! Will this help us to keep ourselves pure? It will indeed - those who practise the presence of God do not fall so easily into sin as others do. Young Christian, do not be satisfied until prayer is a real, living experience in your life. Speak to God freely about your problems and temptations, and about your hopes and aspirations, too. He is your Father and He expects you to share your life with Him.

WITNESSING

Third on the list I would put witnessing, because this is very important. It brings joy into a Christian's life like nothing else will. *"Go home to your friends, and tell them how much the Lord has done for you"* (Mark 5:19). Every one of us must be a witness. Christ has commanded it. Go and tell, He says. A witness is a person who tells what he knows. To know what we know - about sin and hell, and Christ and salvation - and not to tell, isn't that serious beyond words? Paul thought it was. *"Woe to me,"* he said, *"if I do not preach the gospel"* (1 Corinthians 9:16). Do we believe that if our friends die in their sins they will be lost for ever? And that the Lord Jesus died to save them from destruction, and that by believing in Him they will be for ever saved? Then why are many of us so slow to speak about Him? Can it be that we are ashamed? Or just careless? Or too busy with other things? *"You will be My witnesses,"* the Lord Jesus said, just before He left, and soon He is coming back again.

What answer shall we give when He asks why we have told so few? He is coming soon, and *"everyone who thus hopes in him purifies himself as He is pure"* (1 John 3:3). Yes, this also will help us to keep ourselves pure. It will have a good effect in our own hearts, quite apart from the eternal blessing which will come to others when they believe because we told them about the Saviour.

Read and pray and witness, young disciple, and do so every day and you will find yourself living the abundant life that Christ died to give you. Go in for all three in a big way and you will lay hold on the life which is really life (as Paul said to Timothy in 1 Timothy 6:19). This is what it means to be a committed Christian and who wants to be less than that? Jesus Christ, God's holy Son, held nothing back at Calvary, but gave Himself, all that He had and was, for me – dare I hold anything back from Him?

7. CHOOSING A PARTNER

"He will give you the desires of your heart" (Psalm 37:4).

"Do you believe God has a plan for your life?"

"I suppose I do in a vague sort of way, but I wish I was more sure about it."

"What do you think about Ephesians 2:10; does it help at all?" *'We are His workmanship, created in Christ Jesus for good works, which God prepared beforehand that we should walk in them.'*

So before God started working on us, that is, before we were saved, He had planned the good works which we would do. Another verse says that God works all things after the counsel of His will (Ephesians 1:11), and "all things" surely includes the details of our lives. I have no doubt in my mind that God, who is all-knowing, knows what is best for me in my new life in Christ and has planned it beforehand. Of course whether I ask Him to make clear His plan and walk in it, or go my own way and rebel against it, depends upon me, but that is another subject.

Many young people struggle with this problem, but if we get the basics sorted out and agree that our wise and loving God is in control of our lives and that He not only seeks the best for us but is also prepared to guide us into it, we shall feel a sense of peace in our hearts. And if that is true, surely the all-important decision of who my life-partner is to be is one of the primary things that God has planned.

GOD'S CHOICE

Abraham's trusted servant had no doubt about that as he set out on the errand which his master had given him. Not many would have envied him his task, to select a bride for his master's son. And possibly he would not have undertaken it himself if he hadn't been so firmly convinced that there was one young woman who was God's choice for Isaac, and that He would show him who that one was. That point comes out clearly in his prayer, *"Let the young woman to whom I shall say, 'Please let down your jar that I may drink,' and who shall say, 'Drink, and I will water your camels'—let her be the one whom you have appointed for your servant Isaac"'* (Genesis 24:14).

Admittedly the circumstances are different from some of our own. This man was being sent to select a wife on behalf of someone else, and that is not the custom in most countries today. But there are some basic principles from which God obviously expects us to learn valuable lessons. This servant had not the slightest doubt that there was one young woman whom God had appointed to be Isaac's wife and he set out to find that one, with God's help. And if that is so for Isaac, will God do less for you and me? Believing this removes anxiety from the mind, and we can rest in the Lord and wait patiently for Him.

FLIRTING

That does not mean there is nothing we have to do, for there is; but it does cut out flirting, singling out one person after another for particular friendship until we find the one who suits us best. That is unworthy of a disciple of the Lord Jesus, to say the least, and it often leaves a trail of damage in the lives of the those whose affections have been flirted with. A young guy should never play around with the affections of a young woman. He may quickly forget all about it when the friendship is broken, but not so his girl friend. Her emotions are less easily aroused than his, but by the same rule the damage is less easily repaired. Of course, this does not apply to guys only. Girls are guilty of the same thing. If you are in any doubt about the seriousness of it, read Proverbs 26:18,19: *"Like a madman who throws firebrands, arrows, and death is the man who deceives his neighbour, and says, 'I am only joking?'"* Be clear, young friend, flirting is not God's way of finding a partner, and those who resort to it very often end up by missing God's best.

BEGIN BY PRAYING

Back again to Abraham's faithful servant. The first thing he did on his errand was to pray. Every young Christian who is seeking a partner should note this point. When this time comes in your life, begin by making it a subject of earnest prayer. Tell the Lord about it and ask Him in simple faith to make clear to you the person of His choice. If you do that sincerely from your heart and then fulfil the conditions of Psalm 37:3,4, He will do His part and give you the desires of your heart. Remember all God's promises are in two parts, ours and His, in that order usually. If we do our best in doing our part, He will do His best in fulfilling His - and there is nothing better than God's best!

Then what do we do? Sit and wait expecting our life partner to be delivered along with the morning mail? Not at all. In most cases God will bring someone across your path to whom you will feel attracted. This may be an instantaneous thing, "love at first sight" as we sometimes call it, or it may gradually grow in our heart towards a person you have known a long time. But when it happens you will know. And especially if you have been prayerfully asking God about it.

THE IDEAL PARTNER

What sort of a partner are you looking for anyway? Everyone will have their own answer to that question and there may be no harm in having our ideas, for we have to live together for the rest of our lives. But do let us be flexible, for it is not very often that our ideal person turns up. And please remember that *"Charm is deceitful, and beauty is vain: but a woman who fears the LORD is to be praised"* (Proverbs 31:30).

Outward appearance is very unimportant really compared with Christian character. Young Christian men thinking of marriage do well to ponder what God has to say in Proverbs 31 about the ideal wife and mother. And Psalm 112 will repay careful study by any young woman who wants to know the characteristics that God looks for in a man who pleases Him. The fear of the Lord rates high in both cases, and *"the fear of the LORD is a fountain of life"* (Proverbs 14:27).

PULLING TOGETHER

Of course, it's no use praying about someone who God plainly says in His Word is outside of His will for you. Before we go further, let us clarify two points. Firstly, our partner must be a born-again believer. *"Do not be unequally yoked with unbelievers,"* is the simple command of 2

Corinthians 6:14, and there's a good reason for that. In Deuteronomy 22:10 God says, *"You shall not plow with an ox and a donkey together."* These two animals were never to be yoked together. It was not the length of their legs or the strength of their bodies that made them unsuitable to pull together, but the fact that they were of different natures.

That is why an unbeliever is forbidden as a partner for a believer. Their natures are different. The believer has a new nature which loves heavenly things, and the unsaved person has only the old nature which is opposed to God. If each follows the inclination of his or her nature, they will be pulling in opposite directions, and what sort of a marriage would that be? The command is clear: *"Do not be unequally yoked."* It doesn't leave any room for questions or arguments. Light and darkness just do not mix. The believer is "in Christ" destined for heaven; the unbeliever is still in their sins, and if they die in them, they are heading for eternal judgement.

"But if I get married to him I can gradually win him for Christ," argued a Christian girl who was set on an unsaved boyfriend. In reply her Bible class leader asked her to jump up on a table. "Now pull me up," he said, and of course it was more than she could do. "All right, get ready, I'm going to pull you down," and no sooner were the words out of his mouth than she was on floor level again. And that is the way it usually works.

PULLING THE SAME WAY

This brings us to our second point, for 1 Corinthians 7:39 stipulates that marriage is to be *"only in the Lord."* What does that mean? There are three expressions in the New Testament which are connected with one another. Paul says in Acts 17 that all men should seek God, for *"in Him we live and move and have our being."* God is the Creator of all men, and *"He*

Himself gives to all mankind life, and breath, and everything" (Acts 17:25). In that sense all men are *"in God."* Then in the epistles of Paul another expression *"in Christ"* is commonly used. For instance, *"If anyone is in Christ, he is a new creation"* (2 Corinthians 5:17). This is true of all who have accepted Christ as their Saviour. They are *"in Christ"* and in Him they are for ever safe. They will not come into judgement, but have passed out of death into life.

But marriage for the disciple must be only in the Lord, and *"in the Lord"* has a different meaning again. Jesus Christ is Lord. God has made Him so. Lordship involves authority and authority demands obedience. *"Why do you call Me, Lord, Lord, and not do what I tell you?"* asked the Lord Jesus (Luke 6:46). We can see therefore that *"in the Lord"* is an expression used of obedient persons who have acknowledged the authority of Christ, openly witnessed to it in baptism, and have been joined with others to worship and serve the Lord in the way that He has instructed us. This bring the disciple into a church of God, where he is cared for by overseers who are described by Paul as being *"over you in the Lord"* (1 Thessalonians 5:12). We can immediately see that this different from being *"in Christ,"* as one of the members of the Church, His Body, for in that Body no one is over us except Christ who is the Head.

In God, in Christ, in the Lord - the circle is narrowing each time, and marriage for the disciple who is in a church of God is to be only "in the Lord." "But that restricts me! Can I not be free to marry if the person is a born-again believer?" It is true it restricts you, but not without good reason. If it is God's commandment it must be for our good. *"His commandments are not burdensome,"* John says in 1 John 5:3. Let us then examine the reason why the Lord restricts marriage for a disciple to the comparatively narrow confines of *"churches of God"* (1 Thessalonians 2:4).

WORSHIPPING TOGETHER

Marriage, as we shall see in a later chapter, is a very close union, affecting every area of our lives. Husband and wife are joined to one another, not only physically but in the things of the spirit and soul as well. *"Do two walk together, unless they have agreed …?"* God asked in Amos 3:3. He did not stop to answer His question, for it is obvious. And this agreement must reach into every area of our lives if marriage is to be as happy and rewarding as God intended it to be. Both parties may sincerely love the Lord Jesus as their Saviour, but if one is a baptized disciple in a church of God and the other is not, they have to part company on the finest hour of their week.

If there is one time above all others when they should be together it is on Lord's day morning, enjoying the highest function possible to any person this side of heaven, worshipping God at the Remembrance of the Lord Jesus. The most enriching part of married life is serving the Lord together among His people, and if partners are not one in this area of their lives then they will lose out on the best that God has for them. So God is right! He always is. Marriage *"only in the Lord"* is not a commandment intended to restrict us for restriction's sake. It is for our highest good and those who bow to it prove it to be so.

WHAT SHOULD I DO?

One other point before we close this chapter. Occasionally it happens that a young disciple falls in love with someone outside the churches of God. It may not be of their own seeking, but it happens, and they are in a dilemma to know what to do. They love the Lord Jesus and value their place in God's house. What then should they do in such a circumstance? The following advice is offered suggestively on a delicate subject, and anyone who finds himself in such a situation, without having sought it deliberately, may perhaps find guidance in it. First and foremost, do not commit yourself in any way. Keep a tight hold on your affections, always remembering that you belong to the Lord Jesus and in your baptism you vowed yourself to Him for all time. Your first love therefore belongs to Him and nothing or no one must be allowed to take His place.

If on that point you are agreed, invite the person along to suitable church gatherings and introduce him or her to your Christian friends. And then devote yourself to serious prayer. Others will doubtless be praying with you, especially if you confide your problem to them, but be careful to keep a hold on your affections. But you say, "I have fallen in love with him/her; how can I help myself?" Admittedly this is not easy, and I would hardly dare to write this if I did not know that some in the churches of God today are there because their spouse faithfully followed the course I am now suggesting. If this is the partner of God's choice for you, He will work by His Spirit in his heart, revealing Christ as Saviour and Lord.

You will notice that when Abraham's servant sought Rebecca for Isaac he showed her and her family all the good things of his master's. And when they let him speak it was about his master and his master's son that he spoke. He had no other subject. Ten times over the words *"my master"* occur. No servant ever had a better master, in his opinion. Then he looked for Rebecca's decision. *"Will you go with this man?"* *"I will go,"* (Genesis 24:58) she said, and in making her choice that day it was not only to be Isaac's wife but also to serve Isaac's God. The two were bound together. So allow time for the Holy Spirit to work. He will speak about your Master. That is His work. He loves to take of the things of Christ and reveal their preciousness to human hearts. Eventually your friend will make their decision.

And what if, after all, their answer is "No"? I write gently, for I am well aware that this may go deep into some heart somewhere. But ask God to help you, if that happens, to say "No" too. And press on undaunted to serve the Lord in His house, daring to believe that what the man of God said is true in your case also: *"The LORD is able to give you much more than this"* (2 Chronicles 25:9).

8. MARRIAGE

"Let marriage be held in honour among all" (Hebrews 13:4).

A smiling young couple greeted me after a church service. I thought they looked a little shy and I soon knew why! "We are planning to get married in September," they said. "Will you marry us?" When the first surprise had worn off I protested that I had never taken a marriage service. Wouldn't they prefer to have someone with experience? "Not at all," said the budding young bridegroom. "Don't worry about that; it's the first time for us, too!" And so we agreed to be first-timers together.

The happy sequel was that, with God's help, they were properly married, with every prospect of "living happily ever after." And is that not just what God intends? For marriage is one of His great gifts to us, which He has ordained for our highest good. The Bible begins with a marriage and ends with a marriage, and at a marriage feast the Lord Jesus performed His first miracle. So obviously this is a subject near to the heart of God. Perhaps that is one reason why there is so much confusion about it in the world today, for the Devil loves to spoil anything which God has designed for the good of His creatures. Let us get back to the Bible then and find out together what God has to say about it. He conducted the first marriage, and more than that, the idea of marriage began with Him, so clearly He alone can tell us what it is all about.

THE FIRST MARRIAGE

Genesis 2 gives us the delightful account of the first marriage in the garden of Eden. During six days the Creator was busy in creation and after each day's work He examined what He had made and pronounced it to be good. At the end of the sixth day, in which He made man, it says, *"God saw everything that He had made, and, behold, it was very good"* (Genesis 1:31). So it grabs our attention when we read on to chapter 2 and find that in that scene of perfection, before sin entered, there was one thing which was not good. *"The LORD God said, 'It is not good that the man should be alone; I will make him a helper, fit for him'"* (Genesis 2:18).

Adam was lonely. In all God's creation he had no companion, equal with himself, with whom he could commune. And God set about fixing that situation by taking one of Adam's ribs, after He had put him into a deep sleep, and building it into a woman. And then, very simply but beautifully, the Bible says God *"brought her to the man"* (Genesis 2:22). That was the first marriage. Eve was God's finest gift to Adam. The garden of Eden abounded with gifts for him to enjoy, but his wife was unique and special, one who would share with him in all life's experiences, each for the other and both for God. It is still so. *"House and wealth are inherited from fathers: but a prudent wife is from the LORD"* (Proverbs 19:14).

COMPANIONSHIP

In Genesis 1:26 God says, *"Let us make man in our image, after our likeness."* That is what makes man different from all God's other creation. We have been made in the likeness of God, with minds that can reason, hearts that can love; spiritual beings capable of communing with God, and physical beings with bodies to make contact, through our five senses, with the world in which we live. And in all our functions, spiritual, mental, emotional, physical, we need companionship. That is the primary purpose of marriage.

God gave Eve to Adam to be a help to him in every area of *his* life, someone with whom all life's experiences could be enriched by sharing them together. That makes marriage a very high and noble thing. Two people, made by God and for God, joined together so that unitedly they might live their lives for Him. Peter sums it up in one wonderful phrase when he describes husband and wife as *"joint-heirs ... of the grace of life"* (1 Peter 3:7 RV).

PROCREATION

Back again to Genesis 1:28: *"And God blessed them. And God said to them, "Be fruitful, and multiply, and fill the earth and subdue it."* This is another purpose in marriage. God brings two people together that through their union children might be born and the human race continued. It was never His intention that they should be born, or conceived, outside of marriage. His perfect plan is that they should come into the security of happy family life, where there is a father to provide and control and a mother to love and care. The process of conception, growth inside the mother's womb, and birth is wonderful indeed. David marvelled at it when he wrote, *"You knitted me together in my mother's womb. I praise you, for I am fearfully and wonderfully made ..."* (Psalm 139:13–14).

I expect you're familiar with the facts of how life begins. If not, do get hold of one of the excellent books listed in the Bibliography at the end of this book and learn about it in a right and wholesome way. It's a shame that such a wonderful thing as human birth which demonstrates the wisdom and power of God in such a remarkable way, should be clouded in anyone's mind by unclean thoughts. Get hold of the facts as presented by Christian doctors and others who write with God-given knowledge, and you will want to praise God that you yourself have been so fearfully and wonderfully made. And one day when He brings to you a partner in life, maybe God will use you in this marvellous process of bringing another life into being. When that day comes you will praise Him even more.

PHYSICAL UNION

Marriage has a third purpose, for God intends that it should be firmly based in the deep love of each partner for the other, and this love finds its expression and fulfilment in their physical union. It is by this union that babies are conceived, but the Bible is clear that this is not the only purpose for it. Sexual intercourse gives to married people a deep sense of pleasure which God intends for their well-being, and by which they express their love for one another in a special way. This is yet another of God's gifts, but it is only for those who have been joined in marriage.

To indulge in it before marriage is a very serious sin, something which God hates. Let us all be very clear on that point. The world around us cares nothing for what God says. The Bible is a closed book to most people and its commandments are ignored. Men and women live for themselves, and because the sexual act gives pleasure they indulge in it regardless of God's holy commandments and the awful consequences of disobeying them. But every young disciple must be absolutely clear that this is solemnly forbidden by God. The sexual act outside of marriage is called fornication, and when either or both of the persons are married and they indulge in it with someone other than their own partner, it is called adultery, and the Bible says, *"God will judge the sexually immoral and adulterous"* (Hebrews 13:4).

This is a solemn word, for although the act may be hidden from everyone else, nothing escapes God's knowledge. This sin is so serious that He says, *"Sexual immorality and all impurity ... must not even be named among you, as is proper among saints"* (Ephesians 5:3). That is plain. It is so wrong to God that those who belong to Him should not even speak about it in any light way.

GOD'S WORD VERSUS THE WORLD

The world speaks much about it. Probably there is no subject more discussed. It is glamorized in magazines and advertisements, on television, radio and on the Internet. We cannot live in the world without being confronted with it day after day. If we are not on our guard, the way the world thinks may gradually influence our thinking, and cause us to lower our standards. Young Christian, that must never be. *"Let no one deceive you with empty words: for because of these things the wrath of God comes upon the sons of disobedience"* (Ephesians 5:6).

Do not be put off by the fact that the vast majority of people take an opposite view to your own. God says one thing and they say the opposite. But that is not new. Isaiah lived about 760 years before Christ, and he said, *"Woe to those that call evil good, and good evil; who put darkness for light, and light for darkness; who put bitter for sweet, and sweet for bitter!"* (Isaiah 5:20). If we accept God's standard of what is good, we shall be saved from the evil and darkness and bitterness of which the world is full.

LEAVE AND CLEAVE

What God arranges is always best and His commandments are always for our highest good. His instruction regarding marriage stands plainly at the beginning of our Bibles" *"Therefore shall a man leave his father and his mother, and shall cleave unto his wife: and they shall be one flesh"* (Genesis 2:24 RV). Notice the main points - leave, cleave and one flesh. "Leave" means to break with previous family ties, which everyone who knows the person will be aware of. Marriage is never a hidden thing. "Cleave" is a strong word meaning "to glue, or to join fast together" And then, only then, one flesh. I am certain that being one flesh involves far more than the physical act, but I am also certain that this verse alone forbids that act to anyone who has not first of all been joined in marriage. This is a key verse. The Lord Jesus quoted it, and the apostle Paul also on two occasions, and *"a threefold cord is not quickly broken"* (Ecclesiastes 4:12).

In the normal course of events the time will come when you will wait nervously by the side of your best man, or, if you are a girl, will walk down the aisle on your father's arm, and when that day comes you will be deeply thankful if you have obeyed God's clear commands and kept yourselves pure for one another. That it may be so with every one of the Lord's young people to whom I affectionately write, is my earnest prayer.

9. PRE-MARITAL SEX

"The fruit of the Spirit is ... self-control" (Galatians 5:22,23).

"Is my body redeemed, too?" asked a young Christian to whom the idea was new. "I thought it was only my soul Christ died to save."

"Oh no, He died to buy the whole of you, spirit, soul and body. That is why Paul says we wait for the redemption of our body, which will take place when the Lord Jesus returns to take us all home to heaven."

Redemption is a wonderful subject. There are two Greek words used to describe it; one means "to buy out of" and the other "to release on payment of a ransom," as though the Lord Jesus came down into the market of human life, and paying the ransom price of His own blood, He bought us out of the bondage of sin and set us free. And we are free, but not to please ourselves, of course, for Titus 2:14 makes it plain He *"gave himself for us, to redeem us from all lawlessness'* - and 'lawlessness' simply means pleasing ourselves.

We are no longer our own for Christ has bought us, and it is now our pleasure to do His will. Our actual bodies are His and recognising this we present them a living sacrifice, holy, acceptable to God, which is our reasonable service. Reasonable? Of course it is. If He died for me, then I belong to Him. It is as simple as that.

OUR BODIES ARE THE LORD'S

This is one of the strong reasons why pre-marital sex is so very wrong. Paul deals with the subject in some detail in 1 Corinthians 6, where he says, *"the body is not for sexual immorality, but for the Lord"* (1 Corinthians 6:13). Our bodies are His because He bought them at Calvary, and to show that they are His and to seal them for Himself, He has put His Holy Spirit within our hearts. If a Christian commits fornication he uses his body which belongs to Christ to commit this sin, and we can see at once how very wrong this is. Let us be absolutely clear about it. It is wrong even for an unbeliever, for it is against His holy law which the Creator has given for the benefit and well-being of all His creatures. But for the child of God there are more and stronger reasons why it is wrong, for we are in a much closer relationship to God than the person who is still unsaved.

Another reason Paul gives in the same paragraph. *"Your bodies are members of Christ"* (1 Corinthians 6:15), joined to Him in that wonderful union of the Church which is described as *"His Body."* What a terrible thing it is when someone thus joined to Christ joins himself in sin to a person who is not his God-given partner. Only when God joins two persons together in marriage is the physical act of intercourse allowed, never before, and with no one else afterwards, while life sustains the marriage bond.

THIS IS THE WILL OF GOD

This is something sacred and if we go against God's holy Word we shall do so at our own risk. It won't just bring great sadness into our lives but we shall also lose our place in a church of God. Those who have sex outside of marriage have to be put away (excommunicated) from a church of God, as 1 Corinthians 5:9-13 teaches, for they have no inheritance in the kingdom of Christ and God. See also Ephesians 5:5-7. It is true that if there is genuine repentance, the person put away may later be restored, but only after much sorrow - and let us remember that that sorrow will be shared by the Lord. We shall have displeased Him and that's a key consideration with those who love Him.

God's word is plain: *"This is the will of God, your sanctification, that you abstain from sexual immorality ... For God called us not for impurity, but in holiness"* (1 Thessalonians 4:3,7). Sanctification simply means "being set apart," and we are *"sanctified in Christ Jesus"* which means God has set us apart in Christ for Himself. We have to acknowledge this and keep ourselves apart from all that we know will displease Him. Sanctification is a two-sided subject - God's side and ours. There is really nothing complicated about it as long as we have honest hearts and love the Lord. God has done His part and He now expects us to do ours. *"Whoever disregards this, disregards not man but God, who gives His Holy Spirit to you"* (1 Thessalonians 4:8).

We are surrounded today by people who are rejecting what God says on the subject of sex, love and marriage. But this isn't really anything new. Paul's letter to the Corinthians makes it clear that those Christians lived in a similar society. And thousands of years before that, in the days of Noah *"the LORD saw that the wickedness of man was great in the earth, and that every intention of the thoughts of his heart was only evil continually"*

(Genesis 6:5). And the most serious sin of that day was associated with sex. So it is certainly not new. But that fact doesn't make it any less serious.

SOWING AND REAPING

We write bluntly on the subject because we meet it everywhere today and at school and in colleges young people talk a lot about it. And also because seemingly respectable people, who in other things maintain high standards, appear to see nothing wrong in "free love," as they call it. They wouldn't steal, or maybe even tell a lie, but on this point they follow the world. "If we love one another deeply, why shouldn't we express it in this way?" they argue. "If we are both agreed and no one else is harmed, why shouldn't we?" That is the Devil's argument of course. He argued that way in the garden of Eden, trying to suggest that God was withholding from Adam and Eve something that was good for them. God said "Don't" and the Devil said "Do" - who was right?

As soon as they disobeyed they knew who was right. Cringing behind the trees of the garden in fear and shame, they must have wished they had never listened to Satan. But it was too late. The damage was done and all their lives they lived to regret it, and to reap the awful fruit of their sin. *"Do not be deceived: God is not mocked: for whatever one sows, that will he also reap. For the one that sows to his own flesh, will from the flesh reap corruption"* (Galatians 6:7-8). I am writing bluntly to bring God's prohibitions to the notice of all who will take time to read, and to save one another from lives of deep regret.

GOD'S WAY IS BEST

One of David's sons, Amnon, fell in love with his half-sister, Tamar, and he refused to wait. If he had, it seems as though the king would have agreed to their marriage. At least, Tamar thought so. But Amnon and Jonadab, his subtle cousin, hit on a plan to get what he wanted and to get it at once. He pretended to be sick and he asked the king to send Tamar to bake cakes for him. Then against her will he forced her to have sex. He got what he wanted, but did it bring happiness? On the contrary. It says a very shocking thing: *"Then Amnon hated her with very great hatred, so that the hatred with which he hated her was greater than the love with which he had loved her."* How often that has happened in the lives of young people who have failed to discipline themselves before marriage, and in many cases the rest of their lives have been spoiled.

Two years later Amnon was murdered. And what about Tamar? *"Where could I carry my shame?"* (2 Samuel 13:13) she cried. How many young women, sinned against or sinning themselves, have echoed words like that! Why does God use a whole page of His holy Word to recount such an unpleasant and disturbing story? I believe it is to warn us, because He knows how strong the urge can be, and He so deeply longs that we shall be kept wholly (and holy) for Him. I am thankful the Bible is so frank about these subjects. God does not cover sin, but tells us plainly about it. Such chapters stand out as great warning lights shining out over the deep waters of sin, warning us to keep far away.

"How near can you drive to the edge of a cliff?" asked an employer as he interviewed prospective drivers. "About a yard, sir"; "A couple of feet, sir," answered two daring men. "I would keep as far away as I could," answered a third, and he got the job. Keep as far away as you can, young Christian, and then you can claim the power of God to guard you when temptation strikes through no fault of your own.

CONTRACEPTION

Let us say clearly that the sin of sex outside of marriage is in no way reduced by the use of contraceptives. Sin is only sin if you are found out, in some people's view, but surely there is no need to tell young Christians how very wrong that view is. *"Sin is lawlessness"* (1 John 3:4) – breaking God's holy laws. *"All wrongdoing is sin"* (1 John 5:17), whether we are found out or not. There are various methods of contraception offered today, and widely advertised, whereby conception may be avoided; 'mechanical' means which prevent the sperm of the male reaching the womb of the female; and 'medicinal' means, such as "the pill," which prevent fertilisation.

But this is a subject which need not concern you too much until you are ready to get married. Then you and your partner will need to decide before the Lord whether you should use one of these methods to space out your family. Christian men and women are divided in their opinion as to whether this is the will of God or not, so whichever decision you reach, you should not be critical of others with a different view.

ABORTION

Abortion is much talked about today, too. By unsaved people it is being used increasingly as a method of removing the result of sin. Need we say how very wrong this objective is for anyone who belongs to the Lord Jesus? We know that in some countries it is made easier to obtain an abortion because of legislation which allows a pregnancy to be terminated legally, if in the opinion of two registered medical practitioners certain circumstances apply. But let us be very clear that there's no way of getting round the seriousness of the sin of sex outside of marriage. The sin lies in the act, not in the consequences.

"Is there any circumstance in which abortion is allowable for a Christian?" some ask, and it is not an easy question to answer. But we might say that in the opinion of some, abortion may be within the Lord's will if, in the continuing pregnancy there is grave risk to the health of the mother or child; or perhaps when pregnancy resulted from rape; but these are very exceptional cases, and in such events the persons concerned would weigh up the considerations very carefully before the Lord before making a decision. And we would say again that those who hold such a view would respect others who might be strongly of an opposite view.

10. THE SINGLE LIFE

"... those to whom it is given" (Matthew 19:11).

Our writings would be one-sided if we failed to say something about the single life, to which some are called. It *is* a calling, and there are many who accept it as God's will for them, and are happy in it. The Lord Jesus spoke about such people in Matthew 19 and you will notice that He divided them into three categories. There are those who are born that way, and they do not desire marriage. This applies to both men and women. They are happy, completely fulfilled people, serving the Lord in their single sphere, and making a good job of it. Secondly, there are those who *"were made eunuchs by men"* - which refers to surgical castration; and thirdly, those who *"made themselves eunuchs for sake of the kingdom of heaven."* On the other hand there are those who would like to have been married had the opportunity come their way, but it hasn't, and they have to adjust themselves to the prospect of facing life without a partner.

This may bring with it, for a time at any rate, a deep sense of disappointment, which they keep locked up in their hearts, known only to themselves and to the Lord. What a comfort it is that the Lord does know, and understand, and He helps them to make the adjustment that is necessary in order to live a full and complete life in the calling which they now accept as God's plan for them. Perhaps this applies more often to young women than it does to men, although not exclusively so, and in many cases they might have had partners had they been prepared to disobey the word of the Lord and be married to a person who was not committed like themselves to following the Lord.

FOR THE SAKE OF THE KINGDOM OF HEAVEN

Do you think that such people come into the category of those who make themselves eunuchs for the kingdom of heaven's sake? I do, and I believe that they have a special place in the Lord's affections. I believe also that the marvellous promise of Isaiah 56 is specially for them: *"For thus says the Lord: 'To the eunuchs who keep my Sabbaths, who choose the things that please me and hold fast my covenant, I will give in my house and within my walls a monument and a name better than sons and daughters; I will give them an everlasting name that shall not be cut off'"* (Isaiah 56:4–5).

"His understanding is beyond measure" (Psalm 147:5). He knows so well that most of us have a longing for their own home and family and, if in His perfect will He denies them this, He wants them to know that He plans for them something even better in *His* house, and within the security of *His* walls, if they will remain true to Him.

But as I write I realise that this is not easy, and in some cases the disappointment may turn to resentment and to a feeling that the Lord has let them down. If this is nursed in the heart it could do great damage, and may we suggest to any such that they pour out their complaint before the Lord. The Scriptures are full of examples of men and women who came to God with a grieved spirit and told Him all that was in their hearts, and there is nothing to indicate that the Lord was displeased with them. Take Job, for example. *"I will not restrain my mouth; I will speak in the anguish of my spirit; I will complain in the bitterness of my soul"* (Job 7:11).

God did not tell him off for doing so, but He did expect that when he had unburdened his heart he would be prepared to listen to what He had to say. Tell him everything, young Christian. He is your heavenly Father, and He knows how you feel. He has put the desire for love and companionship into your make-up, and if He does not meet your need in marriage, He is bound to meet it by providing some other outlets for your love; not forgetting of course the simple truth that your relationship with Christ will be the provider of all that's desired if you stay close to Him.

FULL GROWTH

Some may have the lurking feeling that an unmarried person is not completely fulfilled, that there is something lacking. Nothing could be further from the truth. Our Lord Jesus lived the single life, and He was the perfect Man. He is God's supreme example of what human life ought to be, for He loved the Lord His God with all His heart and with all His soul, and with all His strength, and with all His mind; and His neighbour as Himself (Luke 10:27).

We are all made with a capacity to love, and the full-grown Christian, whether married or single, is one in whose heart the love of God has shone, and having learned the lesson of daily dying to self and selfish desires, that love pours through them to others. This is spiritual maturity, to which we are all commanded to press on to (Hebrews 6:1) whatever our status in life.

PLEASING THE LORD

The apostle Paul, himself unmarried or widowed, lifts the life of a single person on to a very high level when he writes, *"The unmarried man is anxious about the things of the Lord, how to please the Lord"* (1 Corinthians 7:32). And he uses the very same words of the unmarried woman in verse 34. Those who are single have the privilege of giving themselves fully to the things of the Lord without distraction, and that is something not to be looked down on. Most single people have their own home or one that they share, and the home presents a tremendous opportunity for serving the Lord. Bethany was a home made up of single people, as far as we know, and surely there was no home where hospitality brought greater comfort and cheer to the Master and His followers than that one. So, if the single life is God's special calling for you, ask His help to accept it as being His best and, reckoning that *"godliness with contentment is great gain"* (1 Timothy 6:6), fill all your hours with happy service for Him.

11. THE WORLD

***"Do not love the world or the things that are in the world"* (1 John 2:15).**

"If you are in any doubt about where to go or what to do, a good test is to ask yourself the question, can I take the Lord Jesus with me?" The speaker was a tent leader at a Bible camp and she was answering the question of one of her girls who had recently been saved. Camp was nearly over, and our young friend was sorting out some of the problems which faced her as she went home to live her new life in a family where she was the only Christian. She found it really helpful when her tent leader read with her in John 7 and she found that the Lord Jesus faced a similar situation in His home at Nazareth. *"Not even His brothers believed in Him"* (John 7:5), and to them He said, *"The world cannot hate you; but it hates me"* (John 7:7).

The world could not hate them because at that time they belonged to it, and the world loves its own. Later, those very men believed in the Lord Jesus and became His disciples, and then it happened to them, as to all who believe, that God took them out of the world and gave them to Christ. That is what has happened to you, young Christian. Once you belonged to the world but now you belong to Christ. You are still in the world, of course, but you are not of it, in the sense of belonging to it. Therefore the world hates you. At least, it will if you are true to your Master. It hates Him. He said so plainly. And it will hate you, if you follow Him.

UNDER SATAN'S CONTROL

The reason for this is that *"the whole world lies in the power of the evil one"* (1 John 5:19). When Adam chose to listen to the Devil rather than obey God, the Devil stepped into control and became *"the ruler of this world"* (John 14:30). He is also called *"the god of this world"* (2 Corinthians 4:4), for he claims the worship of men's hearts which belong to God and - as we know - he very often gets it. At Calvary the Lord Jesus did battle with him and, praise God, He won. So Satan is now a defeated enemy, and *"the God of peace will soon crush Satan under your feet"* (Romans 16:20). Then he will be chained up for a thousand years, and finally cast for ever into the lake of fire. He knows that his time is short and he is doing all in his power to oppose God today. So do not be surprised if sometimes the going is hard. The Lord Jesus warned us it would be. *"In the world you have tribulation,"* He said, *"take heart; I have overcome the world"* (John 16:33). If we put our faith strongly in Him and obey His Word, we shall overcome too. *"This is the victory that has overcome the world - our faith"* (1 John 5:4).

THIS EVIL WORLD

Let us be clear which world we are speaking about, for the word is also used in the Bible to describe the world of men and women which God loves and for which He sent His Son to die. The world which John says we are not to love is the arrangement of things around us, its politics, pleasures, society, religion, sport etc., all of which are geared to attract people. And some of it is very attractive. It caught Demas' eye and drew him away from following Christ. And many a disciple has been drawn off course by this world. But it is evil, for God says so (Galatians 1:4). Its works are evil, for Christ said so (John 7:7). And behind it all is the evil one himself, doing his utmost to entice the young disciple from their allegiance to Christ.

So we all have to face the issue head-on. *"All that is in the world ... is not from the Father, but is from the world"* (1 John 2:16), and this takes in all of unholiness and everything that is contrary to Christ in the areas of entertainment, religion and selfish ambition. They are not of the Father, but I am, and therefore they are not for me. "What's left for us to enjoy then?" "Christ" is the answer, and if you fall in love with Him you will want nothing else. This is not a glib answer, and please don't think that we don't understand the problem. We do, and we're well aware that many young Christians find it difficult to make their decision. But I sincerely believe that the only way to tackle the problem is to face it head-on, as James did.

"Do you not know that the friendship with the world is enmity with God?" (James 4:4), he asked in his blunt way. It is one or the other. You cannot be half a friend and half an enemy; one foot in one camp and one in the other. You might try it for a while, but sooner or later you have to make your choice. And better sooner than later.

DO YOU LOVE ME?

It all boils down to the great question with which the Master faced Simon Peter, just before He went back to heaven. *"Simon, ... do you love Me?"* (John 21:15-17). And He asked it three times so that it would sink into his heart. If we love Him it will be easy, and if we don't? Well, we can do no better than pray the prayer a young Chinese friend of mine once prayed, "Lord, make me to love You." Lee Chwan was a newspaper reporter struggling for an existence in the heart of Rangoon's busy Chinatown.

Having recently given himself to Christ he knew that his only chance of survival was a real love for his Master burning deep in his heart. Of course, Lee Chwan had to make a living like all other people and that brings me to a further point. Although we no longer belong to the world, we have been left in it to live and serve.

"I do not ask that you should take them out of the world" (John 17:15), said the Lord Jesus in His prayer to His Father, and then He added, *"As you sent Me into the world, so I have sent them into the world"* (John 17:18). He was sent to shine in its darkness, and so are we. We have been taken out of the world and then sent back into it, so that the way we live may affect other lives. I like the way Paul puts it: *"that you may be blameless and innocent, children of God without blemish in the midst of a crooked and twisted generation, among whom you shine as lights in the world"* (Philippians 2:15). But more about that in the next chapter.

12. THE MEDIA

"I have made a covenant with my eyes" (Job 31:1).

"But the apostle Paul wrote about '*those that use the world, as not abusing it,*'" says one of my friends. "How does that fit in with what you have been saying?" Yes, that is true and it's found in 1 Corinthians 7:31. And it opens up a very important point, for clearly there are some things in the world which we can use to our profit, if we are careful to take out of them what is good and to reject what is bad. Such things as the Internet, social media, TV, magazines and newspapers come under this heading, and in fact, all the media. Most Christians feel that they need to keep up-to-date with the news, but if we want to avoid polluting our minds we must be selective in what we read.

TELEVISION

Television is a prime example of what I am saying. Some useful programmes appear on it, but all Christians agree, and an increasing number of non-Christians are joining them, that there is also a tremendous amount of rubbish, a lot of it unclean and defiling as far as the Christian is concerned. A large percentage of what appears on television is designed to appeal to fleshly lusts, and Peter says plainly that passions of the flesh war against the soul (1 Peter 2:11). If Christians feed their minds on these things, then they will have lost the spiritual battle before they have even begun. So we have got to be selective. Would you believe that it's not too many years ago that a lot of Christians would not even allow a TV to be in their house, because they could see the harm it could do. It makes you think, doesn't it? All the above applies as equally to the Internet as it does to TV, perhaps even more so as there is no monitoring of what is published online at all! So be careful and consider making a commitment to "cut down," if not "cut out."

GOD'S NAZIRITES

I believe that the instruction which God gave to the Nazirites is connected to this very point. We read about them in Numbers 6. Any man or woman in Israel could take the vow of the Nazirite if they so wished, and they could take it for a set period of time. It was a way of expressing their love for God, maybe a thank offering for some particular blessing they had received from Him. Sometimes a person was set apart from his birth as a Nazirite, as Samson or John the Baptist were, but these were exceptional cases. Usually it was a voluntary vow, a person deciding to become a Nazirite of their own free will and simply because they wanted to show the Lord how much they loved Him. And there is no doubt that God greatly valued this. We have only to read in Amos 2:11,12 where God speaks about His young men who were Nazirites to sense the depth of feeling in His heart about them. They were setting themselves apart specially for God, and they were special in His sight.

THREE CONDITIONS

There were three things which a Nazirite had to observe. They must not eat grapes, either fresh or dried. Nothing from the grape vine, from the kernel to the husk was God's clear instruction. Also they were to allow their hair to grow long until their vow was over, and then it was cut and burned on God's altar. And finally they were not to come near a dead body, even if it was one of their closest relatives. When death comes corruption sets in and that would cause defilement - and that was not allowed to happen to the Nazirite because they had separated themselves to the Lord.

There are no physical Nazirites today and such restrictions do not apply to the disciple of the Lord Jesus. But there are spiritual Nazirites, if we may call them that - young men and women who love the Lord Jesus from their hearts and who want to say so in their lives. They present their bodies a living sacrifice, holy, acceptable to God (Romans 12:1-2). If John the Baptist was the last of the Old Testament Nazirites, surely the Lord Jesus heads the line of the spiritual Nazirites, and you and I can get into that line, if we want to.

CLEAN FROM THE WORLD

What is involved? We must at once acknowledge that we are living in a corrupt world and any contact with its sin and uncleanness is going to defile us. So we resolve that, God help us, we are going to keep ourselves clean from the world. Anything unclean is out, as far as we are concerned. Out will go a large percentage of what appears on television, what comes over the radio and what can be viewed online, and through social media. It is just not for the young Christian. God means business. It also takes in many of the books and magazines with which the market is flooded. Cast your eyes over the shelves in many a bookshop and you have seen enough to defile your heart if you allow it to get in. That is the point, of course. We have to guard our hearts, and the way into our hearts is through our eyes and ears. No wonder Job said, *"I made a covenant with mine eyes."* Wise man. We must do the same. By a deliberate choice of our will we keep ourselves from the corruption that is in the world, for the sake of the Master who died for us.

This presents problems, of course, for we live and work in a world which is rapidly becoming more and more corrupt. And let's face it, there are times when we all become defiled. Then we thank God again for 1 John 1:9, and confessing it to the Lord, telling Him explicitly the point on which we have failed, we find that *"He is faithful and just to forgive us our sins, and to cleanse us from all unrighteousness."* Immediately – if we have been genuinely sorry – we know in our hearts that fellowship has been restored.

DENYING OURSELVES

But what of the grapes and wine which the Nazirite was not to enjoy? There was nothing wrong with these in themselves, for when the period of the vow was over God plainly said, *"After that the Nazirite may drink wine"* (Numbers 6:20). It was one of God's gifts to the people of that land. But the point is that while they took the vow of the Nazirite they denied themselves that pleasure. It was not wrong in itself, but God asked them to give it up while they were separated to Him. This is the heart of the matter. *"If anyone would come after Me, let him deny himself, and take up his cross daily, and follow Me"* (Luke 9:23). We are all clear about the corrupt things of the world, that they are not for the Christian. But what about the legitimate things? They are not wrong but they consume precious time.

And we who are the Lord's are to be good stewards and managers of our time as well as of our money. It's nice after a hard day's work to relax in an armchair and watch some good TV. And we need times of relaxation – God knows that and our bodies and our minds demand it. But this is where young Christians who are really serious get a grip on themselves and switch off even when the programme is clean and good. It would be easy to relax for a whole evening, but men and women of God are not made that way.

MARKED MEN AND WOMEN

That is the issue, straight and plain. He *"loved me, and gave Himself up for me"* (Galatians 2:20). Not for my sins in this case, take notice. That is Galatians 1:4. Thank God He did that, too. But this is Galatians 2:20. He gave Himself up for me, and whether He gets me, all of me, my heart, my talents, my time, and all that I have, depends upon my willingness to give myself to Him. *"We are yours ... David, and with you, son of Jesse!"* (1 Chronicles 12:18). They were all for David, and that meant every hour of every day. The crowd had gone their own way. There were few men of this calibre. How David must have valued them! But this will make me different, you say. That's true. There are not so many who will go this far.

But the Nazirite's long hair also made them different. It marked them out among all others as someone who had set themselves apart for God. They had to be prepared for that. But God looked down from heaven and found special pleasure in the devotion of these men and women. The fact that His blessing upon the children of Israel follows at the close of Numbers 6, immediately after His instruction regarding the Nazirites, isn't without significance. If God gets special pleasure, isn't that enough reward?

13. ALCOHOL AND YOU

***"All things are lawful for me; but not all things are helpful"* (1 Corinthians 6:12).**

"The Lord Jesus drank wine, so why shouldn't I?" asked a young person who found it hard to agree with the reasoning of a friend who thought all Christians should keep clear of alcohol. That is a fair question and it deserves a fair answer. There is no doubt at all that the Lord Jesus drank wine when He lived on earth, for He said so Himself. *"The Son of man came eating and drinking"* (Matthew 11:19), and the Pharisees accused Him of being a *'wine-bibber'* (someone who drank wine to excess), so clearly the drinking refers to wine. And when He so amply replenished the supply of wine at the Cana wedding, we cannot imagine that He didn't have some Himself. Wine was one of the gifts God gave the people of Palestine, and in their country the grape-vine grows profusely.

We have to agree that *"wine to gladden the heart of man"* (Psalm 104:15) is one of His gifts to all His creatures. But with the gift God issued strong warnings about its misuse, for as with so many of His gifts their right use brings blessing, but used wrongly or in excess, terrible destruction. *"Wine is a mocker''* (Proverbs 20:1), said wise king Solomon, so obviously there are two sides to the question.

"IT IS NOT FOR KINGS"

"But if God gives a gift surely He intends us to use it?" urges my friend. That is a fair question, too. What does the Bible have to say about that? King Lemuel, whoever he was, had a mother who taught him an oracle, and he never forgot it. She was a mother who wanted the very best for her boy. The son of her womb was the son of her vows. She gave him back to God, and then did her utmost to train him for the high task God had ear-marked for him. And wine was one of the things she warned him against. *"It is not for kings, O Lemuel, it is not for kings to drink wine; ... lest they drink, and forget what has been decreed, and pervert the rights of all the afflicted"* (Proverbs 31:4-5).

The king was called to too responsible a position, too many lives were affected by his decisions for him to take any risk of his mind being dulled by wine. It might cause him to make errors in his judgement, and wine does cause men to make errors. Isaiah 28:7 plainly says so. It was not for kings then, and it was not for priests either, when they were serving God in the holy place. See Leviticus 10:8-11. And the ordinary person who loved the Lord and wanted to demonstrate it by taking the vow of the Nazirite, as we have seen, was asked to separate himself from wine and strong drink. So kings, priests and Nazirites all denied themselves at certain times.

WHY DID TIMOTHY ABSTAIN?

And so did Timothy obviously, for Paul wrote to him, *"No longer drink only water, but use a little wine for the sake of your stomach and your frequent ailments"* (1 Timothy 5:23). Why did Timothy abstain when wine was taken so freely in his country? Maybe it was because he saw the fearful results of its misuse in the lives of believers, and how could he be drinking for his pleasure something that was destroying the lives of his brothers and sisters? Nor did Paul urge him to do so, but only to use a little for its medicinal value. Some in Corinth were coming in a drunken state to the breaking of the bread, and all around him were lives that were being spoiled for God because of the grip that strong drink had upon them.

It must have been prevalent, for so many references are made to it in Paul's epistles. *"Do not get drunk with wine, for that is debauchery"* (Ephesians 5:18). No man could be recognised as a deacon in the churches of God who was given to much wine (see 1 Timothy 3:8). Even older women are not immune to the temptation. *"Teach what accords with sound doctrine,"* wrote Paul to Titus, *"... older women to be ... not ... slaves to much wine"* (Titus 2:1,3).

Notice the word he uses. Slaves! Does it really enslave? Of course it does, if drunk to excess, and it is a terrifying master. How many lives have been blighted and homes broken because of it. Admittedly the Bible warnings are against *much* wine, and the emphasis is upon the control of it. If you are the sort of person who can hold it in moderation, then it must be agreed that there is no command from the Lord to forbid you drinking it. But I must in faithfulness remind you that some have thought they could control it and found when it was too late that it actually had control of them.

THE SOCIAL DRINK

"Oh, there is no danger of that with me," argues my friend; "I don't even like the taste of the stuff. I take it occasionally just to be sociable. There is so much which we abstain from, for the Lord's sake; ought we not to be sociable when it comes to something about which there is no definite prohibition in the Scriptures? After all, Paul did say he became all things to all men, that he might win some. Isn't this one of those lawful things in which we may join in moderation?"

The argument sounds plausible, but I doubt whether it works out that way in actual fact. The person you are trying to win would probably respect you, and the message you are putting over, more if they saw you stand to your convictions and keep to a soft drink. He knows, perhaps better than you, the awful havoc which has resulted in the lives of people who started off with just the odd glass of what you hold in your hand.

WALKING IN LOVE

Be that as it may, there is one other important consideration, and that concerns my weaker brother or sister, for whom Christ died. *"None of us lives to himself,"* (Romans 14:7) and that is the whole point in Paul's reasoning in Romans 14. I may have no difficulty in disciplining myself to moderation, but if my weaker brother or sister follows my example and fails in that discipline, I am not totally without blame. Paul is laying down a principle which covers anything and everything through which my brother might be stumbled; but isn't it significant that he singles out the drinking of wine and mentions it specifically? I believe he does so because its use is particularly fraught with danger. Its power is so strong and its effect so damaging that he names it, and we must all agree with Paul's summing up, that *"It is good not to eat meat, or drink wine, or do anything that causes your brother to stumble"* (Romans 14:21).

We do not teach teetotalism (a complete ban on alcohol) in the churches of God, for the Bible does not command that. We are not opposed to alcohol used for medicinal purposes. Nor do we judge anyone who decides they can partake without stumbling a weaker brother or sister. But in sending out our message to our young people in all the churches of God we raise a strong warning note, and many of us would prefer to take the advice of king Lemuel's mother, *"It is not for you."*

14. GIVING TO THE LORD

"For they gave ... beyond their means, of their own accord" (2 *Corinthians 8:3).*

Would you like to help a worthwhile cause, sir?" asked a pleasant young lady as she pushed her collection box towards an obviously wealthy gentleman. "How much shall I give?" he asked, trying to buy some time. "Give until it hurts, sir," she promptly replied. "But the very thought hurts me," he said, with a twinkle in his eye. Partly a joke, of course, but perhaps the gentleman was unconsciously voicing the feelings of many people when it comes to the subject of giving. For the Christian, giving of what they have to the Lord, that should never be the case. *"It is more blessed to give than to receive"* (Acts 20:35), the Lord Jesus said, and in that brief statement lies a tremendous amount of truth.

When He spoke those words we do not know, but the apostle Paul tells us clearly that the Master Himself said them. And perhaps God has chosen to place them apart from the rest of the teaching which came from the lips of the Lord Jesus in order to grab our attention. We should remember them, Paul says, and if he says so, we should.

ALL GIVING ORIGINATES WITH GOD

It is entirely opposite to the way the world reasons, of course, but that is not surprising, for God's ways are always different from men's ways. But how does giving bring us more blessing than receiving? I suggest it is when the One to whom we give is the great Giver Himself. David is a lovely example of a man who was blessed through giving. Towards the close of his life, when he had gathered an enormous amount of treasure for the building of God's house, he said *"… all things come from you, and of your own have we given you"* (1 Chronicles 29:14). He knew he was only giving back to God a part of what he had first received from Him, and in giving it back he received a blessing in his own heart far greater than if he had kept all the treasure for himself. How rich his life was - not only in worldly treasure but in spiritual riches, which mean so much more.

GIVE, AND IT SHALL BE GIVEN TO YOU

Let us be absolutely clear that God does not ask us to give to Him because He needs our gifts, nor will He be in any way the poorer if we withhold from Him. Not at all. *"The LORD is a great God … The sea is His, for He made it; and His hands formed the dry land"* (Psalm 95:3,5), *"The silver is Mine, and the gold is Mine, declares the LORD of hosts"* (Haggai 2:8). No, God will not be poorer, but we shall be. He asks us to give because He Himself is a giving God. "God is love, and love must give, for it is love's Prerogative, to give and give and give." And God knows so well that if we learn to give to Him it will be for our own heart's good.

"Give, and it shall be given to you. Good measure, pressed down, shaken together, running over, will be put into your lap. For with the measure you use, it will be measured back to you" (Luke 6:38). The Lord Jesus said this and it is literally true. Those who receive most are those who give most.

God entrusts His richest gifts to those whom He knows will not keep them to themselves, but pour them out again in His service. God uses them as channels through whom to pour His gifts, and what a blessing they receive in their own hearts as a result. The Lord Jesus was right. He always is. It *is* more blessed to give than to receive.

UNCLOGGED CHANNELS

The story is told of a foolish Indian farmer in whose paddy fields there was a natural spring that never dried up. His neighbours' fields were dry and barren and he could not bear the thought of his water flowing over his fields and into theirs. So he piled the earth high around his boundary, to keep it all to himself. He ended up turning his land into a bog. God's word is true: *"One gives freely, and grows all the richer; another withholds what he should give, and only suffers want"* (Proverbs 11:24).

"But what's mine is my own, and I can do with it as I please," argued one young Christian. Was she right? Of course not. It was no more hers than the pure water gushing out of the farmer's field was his. God gave it as He does all our gifts, and if we selfishly keep it all to ourselves we shall dam up the supply and do ourselves immeasurable harm into the bargain. Our God is a great giving God, giving all the time - and He wants us to be like Himself.

HOW MUCH SHOULD WE GIVE?

Is there any definite amount we should give? In the Old Testament God asked His people to give a tenth of all that they received. See Leviticus 27:30 and Deuteronomy 14:22-23. That tenth was used to maintain the Levites who served in God's house. But that was not all they gave, by any means. The firstfruits of their harvests went to God, too, and if, for any reason they were especially thankful to God, they could bring a freewill offering in addition. See Malachi 3:8 where it is clear that tithes *and* offerings were brought to God. But none gave less than the tenth, for that was compulsory under the law. We are not under law today, but under grace (see Romans 6:14), although of course we are still under law to Christ. We show our love to Him by keeping His commandments. The work of God is still maintained by the gifts of His people, but how much we give is left to the decision of our own hearts.

"Each one must give as he has decided [RV – 'purposed'] *in his heart"* (2 Corinthians 9:7) says Paul, but link with that another verse where he writes about giving to the Lord: *"Concerning the collection for the saints ... on the first day of every week, each of you is to put something aside and store it up, as he may prosper ..."* (1 Corinthians 16:1-2). There is no doubt that the **purposing** should be according to the **prospering.**

AN ORDERLY ARRANGEMENT

Look again at those two verses more carefully and you will agree that the apostle was teaching that we should give by definite arrangement with the Lord. There should be nothing haphazard about it. This is one of the great privileges of our Christian life and service, and an orderly method is called for. We should decide on a certain proportion of our income, and having purposed in our heart we must keep to it. Some may need to deduct certain expenses in connection with the Lord's work; bus fares to church meetings, for instance; but the point is that whatever we agree with the Lord is now the Lord's money and we dare not use it for our own things.

Young Christian, if you are not in the habit of keeping account of any other part of your monies, keep a careful account of this and make sure that all the Lord's portion goes to the Lord. If you are paid monthly, divide your offering into as many portions as there are Lord's days in the month, and you will have the joy each Lord's day morning of bringing to God both your spiritual offering, some sweet thoughts of Christ, and also your money offering. With both He will be well pleased.

"But won't you be more explicit? Tell us straight what you think a young Christian should give!" Yes, I will be straight with you and give you my convictions on the subject. I do not think that any Christian should give less than Israel were asked to give, and I know that many love to give more. I know also that many have found that the more they give the more the Lord gives to them, for there is an unlimited supply with Him. *"Give and it shall be given to you"* they find to be literally true and they also find that their joy increases as they have an increasing share (small though it might be) in the furtherance of the Lord's work in their own land and overseas. As we all know, the Lord's work is maintained by the offerings of His people. We can have a share in His work by giving back to Him part of what He has given to us. Laying up for yourselves treasure in heaven, the Lord Jesus called it. Surely there is no finer investment than that!

GOD'S EVALUATION

It is striking that one of the few occasions in the Bible where the actual amount of money given is stated is of the poor widow who cast her two mites (small, low-value coins) into the treasury, and the Lord Jesus evaluated that as more than all the rest of the offerings put together. Clearly God values our giving by what we have left rather than by what we give. The Macedonians also come in for special mention and strangely enough they also were poor.

"Their deep poverty abounded unto the riches of their liberality" (2 Corinthians 8:2), Paul says, and they gave beyond their power. It seems as though Paul and his companions tried to restrain them, but they pleaded with them to be allowed to help forward the work of God. Tremendous folk, weren't they? Of course they had first given their own selves to the Lord. That was their secret. Their hearts were His and giving their money was then a joy.

GOOD STEWARDS

This is a great subject, you will agree, and especially for young people who have the excitement of earning their first salary. The shops are so full of attractive things that there is the temptation to live up to our incomes and spend all we received. But we must guard against that. If we look upon all that God gives us as belonging to Him, and ourselves as His stewards responsible to use it wisely, we shall be saved from this mistake. A steward is a person who is entrusted with the care of that which belongs to someone else. Much of what God gives us will be required to provide for daily needs, and that will be increasingly so when we take on family responsibility. But let us make a firm resolve that out of everything He gives, His portion shall be set aside first and God will bless us in return.

"Make me a little cake first," said Elijah to the widow woman (1 Kings 17:13), who was on her way to bake the last little cake for herself and her son. It seemed a bit hard on the surface, but it wasn't, of course, for Elijah was God's servant, and God must always be first. Those who learn that lesson find the barrel of meal never runs empty and there is always some oil in the jar.

15. GIVING OURSELVES

"He was but a youth" (1 Samuel 17:42).

Down into the valley he ran, healthy and fresh in the bloom of youth. If others were scared, he wasn't. This giant had defied the armies of the living God and in young David's view that was the same as defying Jehovah Himself. And that could never be allowed to pass unchallenged. It is true he was only a youth, but if older men were afraid could God not use a young guy? God had used him to save his sheep when the lions and bears came prowling around the flock, so would He not use him now? The memories of those nights were still vivid. He could almost see that tremendous lion towering above him ready to pounce. God heard his urgent cry and sent him special strength. He was amazed himself how he managed to catch him by the beard and strike him until he was dead. If God helped him then, would He not help him now?

OTHER GIANTS

There was no doubt about that in his young mind as he grasped his sling in his hand and ran to meet the giant. Of course he had met other giants before this one. When the grand old prophet came and anointed him with oil in the midst of his brothers, it was whispered that God had chosen him to be king. It seemed a bit hard to go back to the hills and still look after the sheep if he was going to be king. But he decided that if was where God wanted him to be, he would not allow any proud thoughts to spoil him. So the giant of pride was defeated.

Eliab, his oldest brother, was very jealous of him. He thought that *he* ought to be king, being the eldest. And sometimes he could be very cutting in the things he said. But David did not allow that to worry him either. It takes two to make a quarrel, and he was not going to be one of them. So giant temper was conquered, too. He was only young. A stripling, the king called him, and that means someone kept out of sight, not old enough to be in the limelight. But out on the hills by day and night he had had plenty of time to sit and think, and he had not allowed his mind to wander. Deep in his young heart he loved the Lord and the quietness of the Bethlehem hills helped him to get to know the Lord better. He just spoke to God and God spoke to him, and the friendship that developed was something wonderful. God seemed so near to him that he had no fear at all when he faced the lion or the bear.

IN THE NAME OF THE LORD OF HOSTS

And there was no fear this day, either, even though the giant was twice his size. The thought that the giant might win never entered his head. He was meeting him *"in the Name of the LORD of hosts,"* and that Name had never failed yet. So how could the Philistine win? *"The LORD of hosts"* - those are the hosts of heaven. They all bow before the LORD and there are millions of them. They all serve at His command, so why should one Philistine giant cause so much concern? Down into the valley he ran, God's young man, ready for God to use. He was only young, in his late teens perhaps. But he hadn't wasted the years on the hills around his home. The care of his sheep required skill with his sling, and David had trained himself never to miss. And he didn't miss that day. He saw the unprotected spot on the Philistine's forehead and mustering all his strength he aimed right for it. That small, smooth stone hit its mark and brought the giant thundering to the ground.

NOT ASHAMED TO BE CALLED THEIR GOD

"The people who know their God shall stand firm and take action" (Daniel 11:32). So said another man who had to deal with lions. Not one at a time in his case, but a den full of them. Through faith he *"stopped the mouths of lions"* (Hebrews 11:33), God's record says. Who did it - God or Daniel? God, of course, but He worked through a man who had learned to put all His trust in Him. And God is not ashamed of men like that. He links His Name with theirs. He is looking for young men and women like that today. *"That all the earth may know that there is a God in Israel,"* (1 Samuel 17:46) said David. *"The God of Daniel ... He is the living God, enduring for ever, His kingdom shall never be destroyed,"* (Daniel 6:26) said king Darius after Daniel's wonderful deliverance. Two men, but through them the whole earth heard about the God they served.

"Run to and fro ... look and take note ... if you can find a man" (Jeremiah 5:1). And *"He saw that there was no man"* (Isaiah 59:16). Those were sad days. The same unchanging God - and looking for a man but He could not find one.

WHAT ABOUT TODAY?

Will you be God's man or God's woman, to stand for truth and righteousness? If some of the things we have been considering together have been negative, as we have raised God's warning signs and lifted them for all to see, here is something intensely positive. God is looking for men and women whom He can use. Will you be one of them? *"I do not account my life of any value, nor as precious to myself"* (Acts 20:24), said Paul the great old warrior just before he laid down his armour. To love our lives or lose them for Christ's sake. That is the issue at stake. God can use a man or woman at any age, but He likes them young, with life before them. This is your opportunity, my brother, my sister. Don't miss it, or you will miss life's very best.

> "In the glad morning of my day,
> My life to give, my vows to pay;
> With no reserve and no delay.
> With all my heart, I come."

RECOMMENDED FURTHER READING

- 7 Myths about Singleness, Sam Allberry, The Good Book Company
- God and the Transgender Debate, Andrew Walker, The Good Book Company
- The Porn Problem, Vaughan Roberts, The Good Book Company
- Is God anti-Gay? Sam Allberry, The Good Book Company
- The Fight, John White, InterVarsity Press
- Transgender, Vaughan Roberts, The Good Book Company
- Mindfulness That Jesus Endorses, Brian Johnston, Hayes Press
- Training for Service, Guy Jarvie, Hayes Press
- Exploring Issues of Life, Brian Johnston, Hayes Press
- Get Real! Brian Johnston, Hayes Press

ABOUT THE PUBLISHER

Hayes Press (www.hayespress.org) is a registered charity in the United Kingdom, whose primary mission is to disseminate the Word of God, mainly through literature. It is one of the largest distributors of gospel tracts and leaflets in the United Kingdom, with over 100 titles and many thousands dispatched annually. In addition to paperbacks and eBooks, Hayes Press also publishes Golden Bells, a popular daily Bible reading calendar.

If you would like to contact Hayes Press, there are a number of ways you can do so:

By mail: c/o The Barn, Flaxlands, Royal Wootton Bassett, Wiltshire, UK SN4 8DY

By phone: 01793 850598

By eMail: info@hayespress.org

via Facebook: www.facebook.com/hayespress.org

MORE BOOKS BY ALAN TOMS

LOOK ON THE FIELDS: PIONEERING IN BURMA

A fascinating account of the work done by missionaries in Burma over many years, leading to the salvation of many and the planting of churches which still exist today.

WHAT HAVE WE TO GIVE? BIBLE DEVOTIONS FROM A MISSIONARY TO BURMA

Alan devoted many years of his life to missionary work in Burma (now Myanmar) and he was also known for his devotional writing, much of which centred around the person of the Lord Jesus Christ and the encouragement of his disciples. This book contains a brief background to his life and work and almost 140 of his short devotional thoughts.

WHERE IS GOD'S HOUSE TODAY?

Is God is dwelling among men on earth today? Where is His dwelling place? How may I be sure of a place in it? This book was written because believers want to know the answers to these important questions. It looks firstly at the Old Testament - remembering that 'whatsoever things were written before were written for our learning' (Rom.15:4) and that the tabernacle which Moses built is said in the New Testament to be a symbol or parable for the present time (Heb.9:9). As these lessons are applied to what is written in the New Testament, the author's prayer is that God's Holy Spirit will make clear the lessons He wants believers to learn in regard to the worship and service of God today.

ETERNAL SECURITY

One of the concerns and doubts that can plague a Christian is that, although they've been saved by the work of Christ, if they fall back into the world and lose their love for the Lord, they will be eternally lost. That is, they may be saved one day and lost the next'. If this were true, it would surely be better for them to be ushered into eternity while still in the state of being saved. But is it true? Can that belief be supported from the Scriptures?

A SHORT INTRODUCTION TO THE TABERNACLE

Don't have the time to invest in an in-depth study of the Tabernacle? At 12,000 words, this concise book can be read in about an hour - the perfect introduction to this wonderful subject! Explore with Alan the main features and the vital pictures and lessons for Christians today. Topics include: the gate, the boards, the coverings, the laver, the golden altar, the brazen altar, the table of showbread, the lampstand and the mercy seat.

LESSONS FROM ELIJAH AND ELISHA

Alan recounts the major events from the lives of two of the most significant people in the Old Testament and brings out some important lessons for today about faith, trust, obedience, and knowing God's will in the ups and downs of life.

www.ingramcontent.com/pod-product-compliance
Lightning Source LLC
Chambersburg PA
CBHW050753160726
48004CB00002B/542